Context

Context:
Putting Scripture in Its Place

Context

978-1-7910-3209-8

978-1-7910-3210-4 *eBook*

Context: DVD

978-1-7910-3213-5

Context: Leader Guide

978-1-7910-3211-1

978-1-7910-3212-8 *eBook*

Also by Josh Scott:

Bible Stories for Grown-Ups

Josh Scott

CONTEXT

PUTTING SCRIPTURE IN ITS PLACE

Abingdon Press | Nashville

Context:
Putting Scripture in Its Place

Copyright © 2024 Abingdon Press
All rights reserved.

Library of Congress Control Number: 2023952169

978-1-7910-3209-8

MANUFACTURED IN THE UNITED STATES OF AMERICA

In memory of my grandpa
and great grandma
William "Nuck" King and
Wilma "Maw Bill" King.
I am fortunate to have known
and been loved so well by them.

CONTENTS

The Family Bible

One of the staples of almost every house I entered as a kid was the Family Bible. Are you familiar? It was a large, oversized Bible, with an ivory cover, and "Holy Bible" written in gilded letters. It was also placed in a central location, usually on a coffee table in the living or family room, so it would be in regular view. My family had one as well, and even though we didn't read out of it very often (we used our smaller, personal Bibles for study), its meaning was important and symbolic. Its prominent placement signified the centrality of the Bible for our lives, as did the fact that it was a repository of our family history. The dates of our births, deaths, marriages, and baptisms were all recorded in that Bible. In a real way our lives were bound up in and with the Bible.

So, to say that the Bible has been an important part of my life would be a massive understatement. I spent my childhood immersed in all things biblical—I memorized verses, learned the stories, and even carried a Bible to school most days. As I became an adult, I developed an even deeper interest in the Bible. I took courses in undergrad and eventually did a master's degree, which meant learning the languages and studying the world that created the stories, poems, and letters we call Scripture. I have not only given my life to learning about the Bible, but I have also loved the Bible. The work to which I have committed myself has been and is still a labor of love. That's why I wrote the book you are reading right now, because I love the Bible. My sincere hope is that you can sense that love and appreciation as you journey through the pages ahead.

WHY WE READ THE BIBLE

Isn't it fascinating that we are still talking about the Bible, thousands of years after the contents were originally written? I can't imagine that any of the authors of any of the texts within the canon of Scripture had any clue that their work would transcend time and location the way it has. Not only is the Bible the best-selling book of all time (five billion sold), but it has spawned a massive industry of Bible adjacent paraphernalia—wall hangings, coffee mugs, tee shirts, and tattoos, just to name a few. It would blow their minds, and I bet they'd have questions about royalties.

Not only is it the best-selling, but it's also the most talked about publication in print. Whether on social media or in a doctor's office waiting room, when the Bible comes up, people have opinions. Strong opinions. Which brings us to a really important point about reading the Bible: We all have our reasons for doing it.

For some of us, we are trying to get closer to God. That's one of the reasons that we did our "quiet time" back in my youth group days. We were encouraged to go off, alone, and spend time reading the Bible and praying for insight from God about what we read.

For others of us, we come to the text looking for encouragement and hope. We scour chapters and verses looking for something that could be applicable to the particular moment we are in, something that would be just the shot in the arm we need to keep going.

For others still, we come to the Bible looking for something that might inspire us and empower us to overcome the challenges and obstacles we encounter. When we find such a verse or passage, we might commit it to memory or even post it somewhere we will see it regularly, so that it serves as a reminder to keep going. These are all meaningful and valid reasons to engage the Bible.

We come to the Bible looking for something that might inspire us and empower us to overcome the challenges and obstacles we encounter.

Yet, at times, our approach to the Bible can end up being more about searching for passages or verses that serve other purposes. Instead of looking for inspiration or encouragement, we can easily begin to use the Bible as a source to prove our rightness, and of course, others' wrongness. As we will see, this quickly leads to the weaponization of Scripture and this way of approaching the Bible has harmed countless people over the past several thousand years. While it's true that not every reading that is divorced from context is harmful, many of them are deeply so. We'll see examples of both in this book, the benign readings that miss the context but aren't terribly harmful and the readings that have wounded and traumatized people under the guise of being faithful to Scripture. It's so important to both name and reject the latter, and, at the same time, to also offer a reading that is grounded in context.

PUTTING THE BIBLE IN ITS PLACE

Everything and everyone have a place. What I mean is, we are all from *somewhere*, and that place of origin shapes almost everything about us. I am originally from Appalachia, born and raised to adulthood in a community in the hills of southeastern Kentucky and southwestern West Virginia. While I have spent more than half of my life now outside of that community, it still shapes me, my sense of identity, and my understanding of the world. My friend Brad Davis, a United Methodist pastor who is from, and still lives in, my home region likes to say that we are not just *from* this place, we are *of* this place. Every time he says it, I feel it deep in my bones. I am of that place, and I can't be un-of-it.

The same thing is true of the Bible. It's *of* particular places and people. The poems and stories, the letters and laws, are all shaped by the land, the people, and the events that produced them. The Bible doesn't have *a* context, singular, but contexts, plural. Let's spend a few moments fleshing this out more fully.

To begin, the Bible is not a book. It is a collection of books, a library. This particular library was created over the course of about one thousand years, from the 900s BCE to around 135 CE. However, there are some older snippets than that found in certain books. For example, scholars date the *Song of Deborah* (Judges 5:2-31) and the *Song of the Sea* (Exodus 15:1-18) as older than both Judges and Exodus, perhaps by two to three centuries than some of the other sources that make up those books. Think about how much has changed societally and technologically between 1960 and now. In sixty-plus years we've experienced drastic and dramatic transformations of life and how we understand it. Now think about that one thousand-ish year period during which the texts that comprise the Bible were written. How much change occurred? We are not dealing with a single context, but several contexts. During that period the land and people that are the central focus of the biblical narrative, Israel and Judah, experienced domination at the hands of various empires: Assyrian, Babylonian, Persian, Greek, and Roman. Each of these represent different policies and pressures that would impact the Israelite and Judahite communities, and as a result, impact both how and what the authors wrote.

That span of time means we are also dealing with multiple authors of the biblical texts, and some books are even the product of multiple authors representing multiple time periods. This means that throughout the Bible we are hearing multiple voices and perspectives, and they are interacting with one another over the generations. This is why I don't prefer the language of *contradiction* when it comes to the Bible. When we encounter passages that say different things or offer contrasting perspectives we shouldn't be surprised. It's not a "gotcha" moment for the Bible. That's what we should expect as we hear from our spiritual ancestors who are, from different times and contexts, wrestling with the same complexities and questions we are still sorting out today: What does it mean to be human? What does it mean to be a good human? Who is God and what is God like? Why do we suffer? Why do bad things happen to good people? How do we partner with God to make the world a better place?

The reality is within Scripture we are witnessing conversations between generations of our spiritual ancestors, and as we engage and interpret, we are joining our voices within that conversation. No wonder the Bible is called *holy* and considered *sacred*. The entire experience, the writing and preserving and engaging, then, now, and in the future, are holy and sacred tasks. We not only have the opportunity to meet God through these stories in some mysterious way, but also our ancestors and ourselves. I'll say more about the last part, us, at the conclusion of the book.

Not only do individual books, and in some cases specific sections of individual books, have their own contexts, but the canon of Scripture itself is a context. So is how these texts and this canon have been interpreted over generations. When we approach the Bible, we are joining a large cloud of witnesses that have come before us, and we are making our own contributions that will become part of that very cloud of witnesses for future generations.

As I typed those last words I was reminded of my great grandmother. Her name was Wilma, but we called her "Maw Bill." She was a gem of a human. Born in 1919, she was in her sixties when I made my grand entrance into the world. She wasn't just a great-grandmother in title alone. She really was the best. Before I started school many of my days were spent at her house, right next door to mine. She was at my beck and call. She cooked for me. She played with me. She let me do many things my parents would never have been okay with. She was, in a word, amazing. My favorite thing was when she told me stories of our relatives who had passed before my birth. The way she talked about them made them present to me in some way. I had never met them, but I knew them, I could talk about their lives and, in a strange way I still don't fully understand, I knew them.

I feel similarly about the writers of the Bible. They have given me a gift. As they recount the stories and experiences of our spiritual ancestors, they have made them real to me in ways I can barely fathom. They are present, even though they are past. Which means I wrestle with them, ask questions of them, listen to them, and learn from them, even today. Their voices were not silenced when their time here ended. That, I think, is one of the great gifts of Scripture.

A COMPLICATED RELATIONSHIP

My guess is that, if you are reading a book about the Bible, you also probably have some sort of relationship with the text. In my experience as a pastor, I recognize that, because of all we've already discussed, many of us have a complicated relationship with Scripture. That's more than okay. It's justified. The Bible has been co-opted and used to condemn, shame, and exclude people for far too long. This library we call the Bible is the product of marginalized communities, and to use it to further marginalize is the most tragic of ironies.

How does that happen, we might ask? It is the product and result of approaches to the Bible that ignore the context of a passage or story, and instead, whether accidentally or intentionally, then seek to apply it to a specific person or situation. The following are a few examples of that kind of approach.

The *Ransom Note* approach. While the term might not be familiar (I think I made it up?), the practice likely will be. Think about movies in which someone is kidnapped, and the kidnapper sends a "ransom note" detailing the threat of what will happen if their demands are not met. Demands, followed by threat. The letters are often snipped from different magazines, creating quite the mismatched image, all designed to convey both the demand and threat. This is how many people have been taught to read the Bible. Texts are collected from various parts of the Bible and cobbled together, without a thought to the individual contexts of all those passages, and are applied to situations or people, often with an implicit (if not explicit) demand and threat. "Fall in line, or you'll be in trouble with God," is the vibe. This kind of proof texting was honestly the first way I was taught to engage Scripture. We memorized verses and stories, without much thought to how they fit into their own context, or the larger context of Scripture. It wasn't malicious for me, then. It was just all I knew.

This was especially experienced in contrasting theologies about an event called "The Rapture." If you didn't grow up with *left-behind theology* you are blessed and I don't want to introduce you to it here. However, it is an example of this approach to Scripture. A verse from Ezekiel here, a splash of the Gospels or Paul there, and top it off with a literal, non-contextual reading of the Book of Revelation, and you have a *Ransom Notes* approach to *Eschatology* that has become embedded and unquestioned in evangelical theology. When placed and intercepted within their own contexts, the passages cobbled together do not create a coherent *end-times* narrative.

The *Magic 8 Ball* approach. Do you remember the *Magic 8 Ball*? Imagine an 8 ball from the game of pool. Inside it's filled with a liquid and twenty-sided die that contains various answers like "yes," "no," "maybe," or "ask again later." The point is to ask a question, shake the *Magic 8 Ball*, and then get an answer that would help determine your next steps. This leads to a couple different ways of engaging the Bible.

First, it leads us to see the Bible as an answer book. In the summer of 2002, I served on a team at a summer camp. It was a big deal for me, because it was the same camp I attended during high school, and it was during the summer of my senior year that I realized that being a pastor was the vocation to which I wanted to commit my life. That being the case, serving on staff that summer was a huge deal for me. Every morning our team went to an early breakfast before the campers flooded the dining hall, and every morning we participated in what we called "Dropping It." This entailed one of us opening one of those big family bibles I described earlier and randomly pointing a finger at a verse. That was our verse of the day. Sometimes it was thought-provoking. Sometimes it was hilarious. To be sure, we didn't take it seriously; it was for fun. But the reality behind it was that many of us had actually used this practice to try to make decisions before. Who should I date? Where should I go to college? What should my major be? Surely, we thought, there was a verse for that. Right?

Another example of this approach might be helpful. When I was in elementary school my classmates and I discovered that the Teacher's Edition of our textbooks had all the answers to our homework in the back. This led to many, many attempts at getting those books so we could check our homework before turning it in. Many people see the Bible in the same way, that it's filled with answers to the questions life brings. This doesn't seem to be what Scripture is actually doing. The Bible asks far more questions than it answers. The writers of Scripture weren't crafting an answer book but were instead cataloging their questions. They, just like us, struggled with the big questions of existence. At times they experienced some clarity, and at other times they just stood in awe and wonder at the reality of existence.

When we come to the Bible expecting linear and literal answers to our questions we will, more times than not, either walk away frustrated or we will attempt to use the Bible in a way it was never intended to be used. Pulling random quotes from a passage of a collection of books like the Bible, without considering the context, can lead to serious harm to ourselves or others. One of the gifts of Scripture is not that it answers all possible questions, but that it teaches us how to ask good questions, to be open to the mystery that is faith. Placing the passages and stories in context will not always give us answers, per se, but it will often help us learn what questions might be helpful, and how to begin to engage those questions.

The *Hermeneutic of Assumption* approach. *Hermeneutic* is a fancy word that means "how we interpret the Bible." A hermeneutic is the lens through which we read a text and make decisions about what it means. Everyone has a lens—you, me, everyone. It's impossible to not bring with us our understandings of the world and the experiences that have shaped us. The key, I've found, is to be aware of our lenses and how they might bring biases to our work of interpretation. One further caveat— everyone is interpreting the Bible. No one, including me, has the capability to just "tell you what the Bible says." We all interpret the text.

The *Hermeneutic of Assumption* is exactly what it sounds like. It's what happens when we just assume we know what a passage or text means, without paying close attention to the details or the context. One of the most surprising experiences for me has been the times— the many, many times—I have begun with the assumption that I know what is happening in a particular story or text; but once I engaged that same passage contextually a different interpretation began to emerge.

Making assumptions, thinking we know someone or something so well that we approach them without curiosity or wonder, is detrimental to all relationships, even our relationship to the Bible. The Bible is connected to my earliest memories, and yet, as I live into my fourth decade, it still surprises me. I am still learning and growing and finding new perspectives that make Scripture an exciting and three-dimensional experience for me. When we just assume we have it all figured out, when mystery is conquered, we can end up missing the counterintuitive challenge that the Bible offers us, even today.

When we just assume we have it all figured out, when mystery is conquered, we can end up missing the counterintuitive challenge that the Bible offers us, even today.

A WORD OF WELCOME

So, if you come to this book skeptical, you are welcome. If you come to this book frustrated with the Bible, you are welcome. If you come angry, hurt, and unsure if you even want to engage further, you are welcome. You are also safe. What I offer ahead is a recontextualized and de-weaponized approach to several important passages and stories, most of which are likely familiar to you. I wrote this book with you in mind. So often I encounter people who feel like the Bible, because of the way in which it's been interpreted and understood, has been taken away from them. My hope is to offer it back to you. That what was once a source of wounding might be transformed into a source of healing.

In the following pages, as we dig into some familiar passages and stories that have been separated from their context in our interpretation for about as long as we can remember, we will discover the importance of keeping the contents of Scripture in their place. They were created by people who lived in a real time and place, who experienced real pressures and struggles, and who were trying to sort through the big questions of life. Sounds a lot like us, doesn't it? By seeking to ground our interpretations of the Bible in the context of those who created it is the most honoring and loving way we can approach Scripture. It also unlocks a depth and meaning that we previously might have missed. That is what lies before us in the pages of this book.

CHAPTER 1

A More Excellent Way

1 Corinthians 13

CHAPTER 1

A More Excellent Way
(1 Corinthians 13)

THE TIP OF THE ICEBERG

I performed my first wedding at the ripe old age of nineteen, and over the last two decades plus I have helped more couples than I can remember tie the proverbial knot. While I can't, offhand, recall every wedding over which I have presided, there are some that I can vividly remember. One that I'm sure will make that list of stand-the-test-of-time ceremonies happened just last spring. It was a bit unconventional, which always ends up being my favorite scenario. The couple met while working as servers at The Pearl Diver, a great little tiki bar in East Nashville, and wanted to have their wedding there. They rented the outdoor space—a beautiful little courtyard surrounded by tables—and were surrounded by their closest family and friends as they exchanged I dos, vows, and rings. It was a really lovely evening.

One of the requests the couple made for the ceremony was that I read from 1 Corinthians 13—Paul's famous ode to love. They wanted

3

these words at the forefront of their hearts and minds on that day and always. In case you need a refresher, here are those words:

> *Love is patient; love is kind; love is not envious or boastful or arrogant or rude. It does not insist on its own way; it is not irritable; it keeps no record of wrongs; it does not rejoice in wrongdoing but rejoices in the truth. It bears all things, believes all things, hopes all things, endures all things.*
>
> *(1 Corinthians 13:4-7)*

It makes sense why couples would want to hear these words on their wedding day. They are poetic, familiar, and describe the kind of love that would, no doubt, create a long, happy, and fulfilling marriage. That being the case it's no surprise that 1 Corinthians 13 has played a central role in wedding ceremonies for hundreds upon hundreds of years.

However, if we go beyond this specific use of this passage, with the goal to understand why Paul originally wrote these iconic words and why he wrote them to the Corinthian community, it's important to begin here: Paul was not writing wedding liturgy when he wrote 1 Corinthians 13. Further, if Paul knew that almost two thousand years after he had written this letter that a group of people called Christians would elevate his writings to the status of sacred Scripture, and that one of the primary uses of this specific letter would be during wedding ceremonies, he would be puzzled to say the least.

Our engagement with this passage has only been the tip of the iceberg. When we hear chapter thirteen in the overall context of 1 Corinthians a larger image begins to emerge, one that still offers a challenge to the church, and to each of us who are part of it, today. Before we turn to examine that message, let's talk about what kind of text 1 Corinthians is.

SOMEBODY ELSE'S MAIL

Getting the mail is one of my most favorite things. As strange as it sounds, going to our mailbox is something I look forward to every day with great anticipation. It's a kind of ritual for me. The suspense is just so exhilarating. What might be in there today? Did I win something? Maybe there's a check with lots of zeroes just waiting to be opened? That enthusiasm is usually dealt a swift and merciless blow by reality. Usually, my haul is junk mail or, worse, a bill that demands to be paid.

On the rarest of occasions our mail carrier will accidentally put a piece of our neighbor's mail inside our mailbox. Sometimes I don't catch it at first, and I'll accidentally open it before I realize what's happened. It doesn't take long for me to realize that I am not the intended audience for this particular communication.

When we open the Bible and begin to read a letter like 1 Corinthians, we are reading someone else's mail.

When we open the Bible and begin to read a letter like 1 Corinthians, we are reading someone else's mail. Our name isn't on the envelope, and we aren't the intended audience. I am confident that Paul had no idea in his wildest imagination that his letters to various church communities would be collected, elevated to the status of sacred Scripture, and still be read and debated two thousand years after he wrote them. Please hear me on this: I don't mean that Paul's letters have nothing to say to us. They surely do! By hearing these words first within their original, first-century context, we become more attuned to what they might be saying to us today.

With that in mind, here are a few things to remember when reading a letter like 1 Corinthians. First, Paul's letters were almost exclusively occasional. That is, he was writing to address specific situations in communities, not building a systematic theology by attempting to codify doctrinal or dogmatic positions. One of the criticisms often leveled against Paul's writings is that he seems to know very little about the historical Jesus. Outside of a couple of quotations (1 Corinthians 7:10-11 and 11:23-25), one fleeting reference to Jesus's birth (Galatians 4:4), and a multitude of references to his death and resurrection, Paul gives us nothing about Jesus as a person. He doesn't mention any parables or miracles, for example, two things that were central to the stories of Jesus we find in the narratives of the Gospels. Is Paul unaware of such stories? Does he have no understanding of who Jesus was and what he did beyond his death and resurrection?

I find this criticism of Paul a little unfair, because it doesn't take into account what he's doing in these letters. None of Paul's letters were written so that he could flex his theological muscles and share everything he knew or thought about Jesus. Instead, he's writing to address specific issues that are causing problems within the communities, and to encourage them to remain faithful and do good. It would probably have felt quite odd to the recipients of these letters for Paul to begin with "Here's everything I know and think about Jesus as a historical person."

Paul didn't have a settled theological framework that he was trying to impose. If we pay close attention, across his letters, we will find a theology in flux, in development. Paul is very much building the plane as he's flying it, responding to crises in his communities and articulating his growing understanding of the meaning of Jesus and the movement he began in real time. Our letters from Paul come from the cutting edge of the Jesus movement. He is not the elder statesman teaching the orthodox theological position. He's breaking new ground and trying to remain faithful, while, at the same time, trying to hold together communities that were diverse and fragile.

Second, these letters were written to communities, not to individuals. The word *you* is most often plural. That fact is seen in the names we have given to the majority of his writings: Galatians, Thessalonians, Corinthians, Philippians, Romans. Even the short letter of Philemon is addressed to the community in which the recipient belonged:

> From Paul, who is a prisoner for the cause of Christ Jesus, and our brother Timothy.

> To Philemon our dearly loved coworker, Apphia our sister, Archippus our fellow soldier, and the church that meets in your house.
>
> (Philemon 1-2 CEB)

It is important to keep this in the front of our minds: Paul's letters are not instructions to individuals about what to believe, but to communities about how to behave toward one another. If Paul waxes on about something theological, it's because of the practical implications that it has for the community to which he's writing. It's critical to keep this communal focus in mind, especially with the individualistic emphasis of the culture that has shaped many of us.

Finally, these letters would have been read to the assembled community from beginning to end. When we hear the words of Paul in sermons or lessons, they are usually snippets of chapters, like 1 Corinthians 13. Many Christians are surprised to discover that chapters and verses in the New Testament were a brand-new idea when they began to be used in the thirteenth century. So, when Phoebe delivered and possibly read the letter to the church at Rome, she wouldn't have read a chapter at a time. The community would have heard the whole letter read for them in one sitting.

This means that Paul—or any other biblical author for that matter—was not writing small chunks to be taken and understood in isolation. Instead, he was creating letters and narratives that are connected from beginning to end. That being the case a holistic approach, one that takes into account both what came before and what comes after a text, is helpful to hear the larger message being conveyed.

PAUL AND THE CORINTHIANS

Paul's Corinthian correspondence is deeply pastoral. He's writing not as an outsider who has heard some juicy gossip, but as someone known to this community. After all Paul is the "planter" of the Corinthian church (3:6) and he describes their relationship as a parent-child connection:

> I am not writing this to make you ashamed but to admonish you as my beloved children. For though you might have ten thousand guardians in Christ, you do not have many fathers. Indeed, in Christ Jesus I fathered you through the gospel. I appeal to you, then, be imitators of me.
>
> (1 Corinthians 4:14-16)

Paul founded the Corinthian church, but now he is away from them and still seeking to pastor his beloved community from afar. This feels somewhat familiar to me as a pastor in a post-pandemic world. Before COVID-19 hit in 2020, my pastoral role was very much confined to the GracePointe community that gathered each week in Nashville. Sometimes people would reach out from outside the community for pastoral care, but it wasn't the norm. Fast forward to today, and our community is literally all over the world. Zoom calls, social media direct messages, and email allow me to be a pastor to anyone who needs me, regardless of zip code. That technology would have made Paul's job much easier. In the early 50s CE, however, Paul put pen to papyrus to guide his communities from afar.

It's evident from the letter that what we call "first" Corinthians, isn't. He reminds the community that he had addressed certain issues in a previous letter (5:9), and apparently, they had responded to that correspondence with a letter of their own, asking for clarity and raising new issues for which they needed pastoral instruction (7:1). This letter is ultimately Paul's attempt to address a church community that was in deep division and controversy by reminding them of what he'd previously taught them, and, more importantly, calling them to prioritize caring for one another.

THE WHEELS ARE COMING OFF

Not only could Paul not have imagined that his letters would achieve the status of sacred Scripture, but neither could the church at Corinth. If they could have, they no doubt would have said, "Sheesh, Paul! You didn't have to air our dirty laundry for untold future generations to see!" But that's just what he does. It becomes evident pretty quickly that the wheels are coming off of the Corinthian community in several different ways.

While he begins by calling them saints and expressing his gratitude for them, Paul doesn't waste much time getting to the point.

Now I appeal to you, brothers and sisters, by the name of our Lord Jesus Christ, that all of you be in agreement and that there be no divisions among you but that you be knit together in the same mind and the same purpose. For it has been made clear to me by Chloe's people that there are quarrels among you, my brothers and sisters.

(1 Corinthians 1:10-11)

How popular are Chloe and her people right now? Can you imagine the side-eyes they received when the reader of Paul's letter read those lines? They've tattled to Paul about how divided the community in Corinth has become, and that division is threatening to tear them apart. The central problem that Paul addresses in 1 Corinthians can be summed up in one word: *hierarchy*. In his absence, the Corinthian community began to function more like the Greco-Roman culture around them than the countercultural Kingdom movement that began with Jesus. Paul's understanding of the Kingdom project of Jesus was one of radically inclusive egalitarianism.

Paul's understanding of the Kingdom project of Jesus was one of radically inclusive egalitarianism.

In an earlier letter to the churches in Galatia Paul included words that were light years ahead of his time that sum up his understanding of what Jesus was doing: "There is neither Jew nor Greek; there is neither slave nor free; nor is there male and female, for you are all one in Christ Jesus" (Galatians 3:28 CEB).

It's believed by scholars that this could be an early baptismal creed which that have been recited as new converts joined the Jesus movement. As they entered into and emerged from the waters of baptism, they were becoming part of a new kind of community, one that transgressed and transcended the barriers to full belonging that defined the larger Roman world. As a result, what set these early Jesus communities apart was their aversion to being divided up in hierarchies that mirrored the society as a whole. The problem in Corinth was those old ways of seeing and ordering the world were seeping into the life of the church.

HAS CHRIST BEEN DIVIDED?

Corinth had an embarrassment of riches when it comes to preachers. In fact, they had so many charismatic teachers that it became a dividing issue in the community, and Chloe's people raised the alarm to Paul.

> For it has been made clear to me by Chloe's people that there are quarrels among you, my brothers and sisters. What I mean is this: that each one of you says, "I belong to Paul," or "I belong to Apollos," or "I belong to Cephas," or "I belong to Christ." Has Christ been divided? Was Paul crucified for you? Or were you baptized in the name of Paul?
>
> (1 Corinthians 1:11-13)

Apparently, the Corinthians were ranking preachers and taking sides. It's interesting that celebrity culture in the church isn't just a contemporary problem. The Corinthian church was being divided and becoming entrenched around specific voices. The problem isn't that people had preferences, but that the preferences were creating a gulf of separation between members of the community. The result is the institution of a hierarchy of leadership that prioritized the messenger over the message and created a sense of competition within the church.

This wasn't just a Corinthian problem. Toward the end of Jesus's public activity in Luke we are invited into a scene in which the disciples display a total misunderstanding of what greatness truly is.

> *A dispute also arose among them as to which one of them was to be regarded as the greatest. But he said to them, "The kings of the gentiles lord it over them, and those in authority over them are called benefactors. But not so with you; rather, the greatest among you must become like the youngest and the leader like one who serves. For who is greater, the one who is at the table or the one who serves? Is it not the one at the table? But I am among you as one who serves.*
>
> (Luke 22:24-27)

Paul's response to the Corinthian celebrity culture is the same as Jesus's to his disciples. He calls them to see both himself and Apollos, and by extension any other voice in the community, as people fulfilling the role they had been given.

> *For when one says, "I belong to Paul," and another, "I belong to Apollos," are you not all too human?*
>
> *What then is Apollos? What is Paul? Servants through whom you came to believe, as the Lord assigned to each. I planted, Apollos watered, but God gave the growth.*
>
> (1 Corinthians 3:4-6)

Each person who led and served the community was just doing the work they'd been given to do. The point wasn't the individual personality, but the good work being done to nurture and care for this fledgling community. Instead of seeing others as rivals or threats, Paul invites the Corinthians to see them as co-workers in caring for the community's well-being. The cracks of division will only grow from here.

WHAT KIND OF MEAL IS THIS?

Not only were the members of the Corinthian church taking sides in terms of leaders, but they were also making distinctions between themselves economically. From the beginning, eating had been central to the movement Jesus started. Food was so central to what he was doing that it earned him a bit of a reputation—some apparently called him a "glutton and a drunkard" (Matthew 11:19). The way Jesus conducted meals was radical and likely got him into trouble. In the ancient world meals were a microcosm of the macrocosm, much like a middle school lunchroom can be.

Those middle school years can be brutal, can't they? It's an awkward age, and fitting in is the most important thing, probably ever, and lunch is a crucial piece of getting it right. Specifically, choosing where to sit in the cafeteria isn't just about where you'll eat, but about where you'll rank on the social ladder. The ancient world was quite similar. You only ate with those of similar wealth and class, and women were not allowed to eat at the table with the men.

Enter the Jesus movement, summed up as we've seen in Paul's statement in Galatians 3 about the lack of hierarchy in the communities. There were no distinctions between ethnicity, gender, or socioeconomic status. The organizational chart was flat. That's because, for Jesus (and Paul), meals weren't just utilitarian opportunities to refuel, they were about enacting the kingdom of God on earth. The nowness and hereness of the Kingdom was not a theory, but a practical matter of doing justice. One key way that justice could be done is to ensure that people received their daily bread. Meals, then, were about sustenance and celebration. They filled stomachs with food and hearts with joy and hope. The meal practice of the early church was a declaration that a new way to be human was here.

You can imagine, then, the frustration when Paul found out that the Corinthians had turned their meal practice into an opportunity to divide the community based on economic status.

> *Now in the following instructions I do not commend you, because when you come together it is not for the better but for the worse. For, to begin with, when you come together as a church, I hear that there are divisions among you, and to some extent I believe it. Indeed, there have to be factions among you, for only so will it become clear who among you are genuine. When you come together, it is not really to eat the Lord's supper. For when the time comes to eat, each of you proceeds to eat your own supper, and one goes hungry and another becomes drunk. What! Do you not have households to eat and drink in? Or do you show contempt for the church of God and humiliate those who have nothing? What should I say to you? Should I commend you? In this matter I do not commend you!*
> (1 Corinthians 11:17-22)

Can't you just feel the exasperation coming through Paul's pen? The Corinthians have taken a sacred act of belonging and inclusivity and turned it into another opportunity to divide the community. Instead of a celebration of the kingdom of God, their meals have become an opportunity to reinforce the hierarchies of empire. The practical effect was harm being done to the community members without access to regular food. Paul says their abuse of the common meal was leading to real world consequences: "For this reason many of you are weak and ill, and some have died" (1 Corinthians 11:30).

Paul isn't referring to those abusing the meal here, but the reality they are creating with their hierarchy. Some members are not getting enough nourishment, while many who know only abundance are enjoying lavish meals. The divide in the community deepens further.

GIFTED WITH A COMPETITIVE SPIRIT

The final issue dividing the Corinthian church is that of spiritual gifts. By this point you might not be surprised, but they had turned the gifts of the Spirit into another attempt to compete and create hierarchy and division within the community.

> Now concerning spiritual gifts, brothers and sisters, I do not want you to be ignorant...

> Now there are varieties of gifts but the same Spirit, and there are varieties of services but the same Lord, and there are varieties of activities, but it is the same God who activates all of them in everyone. To each is given the manifestation of the Spirit for the common good. To one is given through the Spirit the utterance of wisdom and to another the utterance of knowledge according to the same Spirit, to another faith by the same Spirit, to another gifts of healing by the one Spirit, to another the working of powerful deeds, to another prophecy, to another the discernment of spirits, to another various kinds of tongues, to another the interpretation of tongues. All these are activated by one and the same Spirit, who allots to each one individually just as the Spirit chooses.

> (1 Corinthians 12:1, 4-11)

Why be so concerned with who received which gift, Paul asks, when they all come from the same Spirit? Why turn this into a competition, when you could instead use your gifts for the encouragement and support of the community? The issue here isn't that people within the church want equality; it's that certain members want superiority. They want to have the best preacher, the best food, and the best spiritual gift. In short, they want to feel like they are better, and more important, than others.

Paul then calls them to remember what this community is, what (or who) it represents by reminding the Corinthians that they, as individuals, are part of something larger. "You are the body of Christ," he writes, "and individually members of it" (12:27). This isn't a competition to see who received the "best gift," or who has access to the most economic or ecclesiastical power, but an opportunity to use whatever ability and resources they have been given to do good and care for one another. In fact, he argues, they are only ultimately harming themselves when they create such division, because they are intrinsically connected as community. As Christ's body, interconnected and interdependent, to exclude, marginalize, and enforce hierarchy against one group ultimately robs the whole of the gifts that they bring to strengthen and energize the community.

This diversity-working-in-unity is described by Paul as God's intention for the community. He reminds them that it is God, after all, who dreamed up both the gifts and their distribution.

> And God has appointed in the church first apostles, second prophets, third teachers, then deeds of power, then gifts of healing, forms of assistance, forms of leadership, various kinds of tongues. Are all apostles? Are all prophets? Are all teachers? Do all work powerful deeds? Do all possess gifts of healing? Do all speak in tongues? Do all interpret? But strive for the greater gifts. And I will show you a still more excellent way.
>
> (1 Corinthians 12:28-31)

Embracing God's diversity is key for Paul, and it leads him to describe a "greater gift" and a "still more excellent way" that will, if allowed, guide the community in their life together. "Word nerds" (like me) will appreciate that the word Paul uses that is translated "more excellent" by the NRSVue is the Greek word *hyperbole*. It's from this word that we get the English word of the same. In English *hyperbole* refers to speech that is full of exaggeration. The ancient Greek was a combination of two words that, together, mean "to throw beyond." This isn't exaggeration but a metaphor for something that is beyond measure, excellent, and superior.

Paul then begins to unpack the "more excellent way" he envisions for this community:

> *If I speak in the tongues of humans and of angels but do not have love, I am a noisy gong or a clanging cymbal. And if I have prophetic powers and understand all mysteries and all knowledge and if I have all faith so as to remove mountains but do not have love, I am nothing. If I give away all my possessions and if I hand over my body so that I may boast but do not have love, I gain nothing.*
>
> (1 Corinthians 13:1-3)

Love is the transformative ingredient that makes everything else work.

I imagine this must've been hard to hear for the Corinthian community. They had entrenched themselves, dug in their heels, and insisted that some people and some gifts were more meaningful and significant than others. Yet here, with a few strokes of a pen, Paul had laid bare the absurdity of their internal competition. Regardless of gifting or ability, or for that matter how publicly or extravagantly one practices good deeds, unless love is the filter through which they are done, Paul says, it's all just a bunch of empty noise. Love is the transformative ingredient that makes everything else work. But you may be asking, what is love? What does it mean? Paul doesn't leave us wondering long.

WHAT KIND OF LOVE?

The word *love* in English is a kind of blanket term. Here's what I mean: If I say "I love you" to someone the intended meaning of my usage of *love* will be understood based on my relationship to the person or people with whom I am talking. For example, if it's my wife I'm talking to, *love* carries a specific meaning that is different than if I am saying "I love you" to my kids. Again, *love* carries a different connotation when I say it to my parents than it does when I say it to or about my church community. In English the word *love* does a lot of heavy lifting. In Greek, the language in which the New Testament was written, there were multiple words for *love*, each of which expressed the specific meaning that was intended. All can be translated as *love*, but they all have different directions and meanings. Let's briefly explore four of these words, and by doing so we will begin to grasp the significance of Paul's word choice in 1 Corinthians 13.

One of the words for *love* in ancient Greek is *eros*. It's the source of words in English like *erotic*, so it will come as no surprise that this word speaks of a sensual, passionate love. Then there's *philia*, which refers to the love shared in friendship. This usage is reflected in the city name *Philadelphia*, which combines this idea of love with the word for *sibling*. Third, we have the word *storge*, which refers to familial affection—the kind of love that is shared and experienced between parents and children for example. Finally, there is *agape*. This love is selfless, and comes from another word, *agapao*, which means "to welcome, to love dearly." *Agape* is the word associated with the love of God in the emerging Jesus tradition, of which Paul is a part. It also came to be a defining approach to the kind of community the early church experienced. These communities centered on *agape* meals or feasts—gatherings that were egalitarian celebrations of the kingdom of God through the sharing of food, drink, and resources. *Agape* is a love that is extravagantly hospitable, self-giving, and generous. It is also the word chosen by Paul to articulate his vision of how a community like the Corinthian church should relate to one another, with a love that imitates the love of God.

A CRASH COURSE IN SELF-GIVING LOVE

After Paul compares all the power and success (for which many of the Corinthians had been grasping) to noise and nothingness without love, he turns to describe the essence of the *agape* kind of love he is centering. Let's revisit his words once again through this lens we've acquired:

> *Love is patient; love is kind; love is not envious or boastful or arrogant or rude. It does not insist on its own way; it is not irritable; it keeps no record of wrongs; it does not rejoice in wrongdoing but rejoices in the truth. It bears all things, believes all things, hopes all things, endures all things.*
>
> (1 Corinthians 13:4-7)

It's worth pointing out a couple of the attributes of *agape* that Paul mentions here. He begins with patience, but that really doesn't fully capture the entire meaning of the word μακροθυμέω. It's not just about patience, but "to be of a long spirit," and "not to lose heart." For Paul, *agape* has stick-with-it-ness that "endures all things," something this fractured and strained community will need moving forward.

Another interesting descriptor Paul uses is that *agape* "does not rejoice in wrongdoing." That might lead us to believe that he's talking about how love doesn't misbehave, but it's actually deeper than that.

He says that love does not rejoice at ἀδικία, which is better translated as *injustice*. Love, the self-giving *agape* that emanates from God, is concerned with justice being done, on earth as it is in heaven. How can we claim to love our siblings, Paul might ask, when we gather and indulge ourselves at a feast of the best food and drink, while leaving nothing for those among us who are hungry? The claim to love, without being combined with the pursuit of justice, falls far short of the kind of love Paul is describing.

Finally, *agape* love is to "bear all things." What does it mean for love to *bear all things*? Interestingly, the Greek word here, στέγω, means "to cover," and is connected to the word for "roof." Love provides the safety of cover, a shelter against the elements. It would stand to reason that love also creates the context for rest and healing.

If it hasn't been obvious up to this point, Paul closes this section by drawing direct connections between *agape* love and the Corinthian context.

> Love never ends. But as for prophecies, they will come to an end; as for tongues, they will cease; as for knowledge, it will come to an end. For we know only in part, and we prophesy only in part, but when the complete comes, the partial will come to an end. When I was a child, I spoke like a child, I thought like a child, I reasoned like a child. When I became an adult, I put an end to childish ways. For now we see only a reflection, as in a mirror, but then we will see face to face. Now I know only in part; then I will know fully, even as I have been fully known. And now faith, hope, and love remain, these three, and the greatest of these is love.
>
> (1 Corinthians 13:8-13)

Agape love doesn't end, Paul writes, but all the things that are creating division and hierarchies among the Corinthians will end—they have an expiration date. The journey toward maturity involves taking those long, uncomfortable looks in the mirror to discover how our communities look like *agape* love, and also the places where we have more work to do. Ultimately, for Paul, if the Corinthians could understand that love was the bedrock upon which everything else rested, then the petty squabbles, selfishness, and ego that was currently fracturing their fellowship would be seen as the childish waste of time that it really was. When *agape* love is the center and focus of the community the competitive impulse that had overtaken the Corinthians would be transformed into cooperation and care for the common good—not just for the individual, but for the whole of the community.

1 CORINTHIANS 13 TODAY

As I reflect on what 1 Corinthians 13 might mean for us today, I can't help but, once again, be transported back to the courtyard at the *Pearl Diver* in East Nashville. On that gorgeous spring evening I read those words because they described the kind of love the couple wanted to be the foundation of their relationship with one another. That is a wonderful goal for any relationship. Yet, there is so much more going on here, isn't there?

As we've seen, Paul wasn't attempting to create flowery wedding liturgy, but to call the entirety of a community to live differently, together. The purpose was to offer both a diagnosis and a cure. The diagnosis was evident: the hierarchies and divisions present in the Corinthian church meant that love was not guiding their life as a community. The cure was also evident: allowing love to become the north star that would guide the community's interactions and decisions. Two thousand years later, that cure is still desperately needed in our world and in the church.

I remember an exercise we did in my youth group when I was in high school with this passage. Our leaders told us to read the verses that described love and, instead of saying *love*, we should say our own names instead. "Josh is patient, Josh is kind, etc." The point was that, if it seemed a bit off, we might have some things on which we needed to work. It was an illuminating exercise, it just didn't go far enough. After all, the point of this text isn't found solely at the individual level, but at the communal. If we allow this vision of love to become our litmus test it must be applied not just to our individual lives, but to our lives as communities as well.

What would happen if love was both the end and the means?

While each of our communities face their own unique contexts and challenges, perhaps there is one blanket application we can make from this passage: What would happen if love was both the end and the means? What would our communities be like if this vision of love was not only our goal but also the ethic that shaped our approach to life together? How would that make our decisions easier? How might it also make some decisions way harder for us? Would it change the way we budget and spend our resources? How would we use our facilities? Who would we welcome that we've been excluding? If we were to overlay Paul's description of *agape* love onto our communities, where would we find congruence? Can we also imagine where we might have work to do?

In my work I talk with people from all over the world who are processing the agony of church hurt and trauma. A common sentiment is that, while purporting itself to be a safe place, churches in far too many instances end up being driven by celebrity, wealth, and competition—just like the Corinthians.

"I thought it would be different," they lament.

I have been around long enough to share that same longing, and I bet you know it too. First Corinthians 13 is not simply Paul waxing romantic, but a beautifully articulated vision of who we, and our communities, could be if we allowed love to be our north star. May we all embrace this more excellent way.

CHAPTER 2

"Your People Will Be My People"

Ruth 1:16 CEB

CHAPTER 2

"Your People Will Be My People"
(Ruth 1:16 CEB)

A FINAL EMBRACE

Roughly four thousand years ago, disaster fell upon the Lajia community in northwestern China. While there is debate among archaeologists about the cause—many believe it was an earthquake that triggered flooding of the Yellow River and the surrounding mountain gullies—the tragic result was an outburst flood that destroyed an entire community. Like Pompeii, there was no time to prepare or react. The end came swiftly and suddenly for the people of Lajia. The flooding unleashed mudslides that buried the entire site in up to 125 feet of mud and sediment, freezing them forever in their last moments.

The site began to be excavated in 1999, and over time archaeologists have made several interesting discoveries, the most interesting of which might be that of the skeletons of an adult woman and a child entangled in an embrace. Headlines, like this one from the *Daily Mail*, announced the discovery: "Enduring love: 4,000-year-old skeletons of mother and child are found locked in dying embrace in 'China's Pompeii' that was wiped out by earthquake."

Things that happen in the distant, ancient past can often be hard for us to relate to.

Things that happen in the distant, ancient past can often be hard for us to relate to. After all, it happened so long ago that the emotional impact has been lost. Yet, there's something about this—this woman holding this child in their last moments—that rehumanizes this long-since-gone community. It makes me think of my own children, and my desire to keep them safe and secure. This woman and child make the past feel extraordinarily present.

Curiously, scientists discovered that one of the major assumptions about this mother-child pair was, in fact, wrong. They aren't mother and child. DNA testing revealed that there is no matrilineal connection between the two. So, who is she, this woman who held and no doubt comforted this child in their final moments? Archaeologists don't know. Perhaps she's an aunt, or a family friend. Maybe she was nearby and scooped the child up in one last act of heroism, trying to find safety. We are left to our imaginations to reconstruct how it is that the two of them came to be in this embrace at the end.

When I stumbled upon this story I immediately thought of Ruth. The short book about her in the Hebrew Scriptures depicts a woman of similar courage and compassion, someone who embraced another in a time of disaster and displayed great courage in the face of uncertainty. For many of us, our experience with her story can be summed up in a beautiful declaration of commitment and faithfulness attributed to Ruth early in the book:

"Don't urge me to abandon you, to turn back from following after you. Wherever you go, I will go; and wherever you stay, I will stay. Your people will be my people, and your God will be my God. Wherever you die, I will die, and there I will be buried. May the LORD do this to me and more so if even death separates me from you."

(Ruth 1:16-17 CEB)

Like 1 Corinthians 13, we often hear these words during a wedding ceremony, and it's not a surprise. They are fitting words to describe the level of commitment being expressed. Also, like 1 Corinthians 13, the context in which Ruth says these words is more complex than we usually understand. What new layers of meaning might emerge for us if we heard these words again within the larger context of Ruth and the cultural backdrop in which it was written? Let's find out together.

ORIENTING OURSELVES TO RUTH WITHIN THE HEBREW BIBLE

Before we jump into the story the Book of Ruth is telling, let's begin by orienting ourselves to the book itself and where it's placed within the biblical canon. In the Septuagint (the Greek translation of the Hebrew Bible) and the Christian canon Ruth is placed in between the books of Judges and 1 Samuel. This placement is due to the opening lines of the book that place the setting of Ruth in the days of the Judges: "In the days when the judges ruled" (Ruth 1:1a).

Here is a brief overview of where Ruth fits within the canon of the Hebrew Bible. One of the names for the Hebrew Bible is the *TANAKH*, with the TNK each representing one of the three main sections that make up the canon. First, there is the *Torah*, or Instruction, the contains the first five books: Genesis, Exodus, Leviticus, Numbers, and Deuteronomy. These books are about Israel's origins and the legal code. Next, we have the *Nevi'im*, or Prophets. In the *TANAKH* the Prophets are divided up into the "Former Prophets," which includes Joshua, Judges, Samuel, and Kings, and the "Latter Prophets," Isaiah, Jeremiah, Ezekiel, and the "Book of the Twelve" (called the "Minor Prophets" by many Christians). You will notice in that ordering, Ruth is not present between Judges and 1 Samuel. In the Hebrew canon Ruth, called *Megillat Ruth* or "the scroll of Ruth," is one of five scrolls (or *megillot*, in Hebrew) that comprise the *Ketuvim*, or "Writings" section of the Hebrew Scriptures. This section contains Poetic Books (Psalms, Proverbs, and Job), Five Megillot (Song of Songs, Ruth, Lamentations, Ecclesiastes, and Esther), and finally the remaining books of Daniel (not in the Prophets in the Hebrew canon), Ezra-Nehemiah, and Chronicles.

RUTH, TORAH, AND SHAVUOT

Ruth has a connection with a specific festival on the Jewish liturgical calendar. Shavuot, also called the "Feast of Weeks," or "Pentecost," happens fifty days after Passover, and is primarily focused on two things. First, it is an agricultural festival that celebrates the grain harvest, and second, it remembers the giving of the Torah to

Israel on Mount Sinai. Both of these are important to the Book of Ruth, the agricultural competent explicitly and the Torah component implicitly.

The connections of the Book of Ruth to Shavuot as a grain festival are evident. As we will see, it is Ruth's bold action during the grain harvest that transforms the situation in which she and Naomi, her mother-in-law, find themselves. However, there is a strong undercurrent linking the story of Ruth to the Torah.

One such link between Ruth, Torah, and Shavuot is how both Israel and Ruth voluntarily embrace the demands of Torah as their own. When the Israelites arrived at Mount Sinai, after their liberation from bondage in Egypt, God invited them into a covenant relationship. The people embrace this invitation at Mount Sinai and commit themselves to this covenant with the Divine (see Exodus 19).

In similar fashion, Ruth, in her declaration of fidelity to Naomi, embraces Naomi's God, people, and land in an act of voluntary commitment. Unlike Israel during their wandering of the wilderness, Ruth will be an example of faithfulness to the covenant to which she had committed herself.

Additionally, the central theme found within the Book of Ruth is that of *hesed*. *Hesed* is a Hebrew word that can be translated as "loving kindness," "covenant loyalty," "faithful love," "steadfast love," or even just simply as "kindness," "goodness," or "mercy." *Hesed* is love and benevolence that are extended without any obligation. It is a beautiful expression of kindness and grace.

In the Hebrew Bible *hesed* appears more than 240 times and can come from both divine and human sources. Again and again, we see God as a generous source of *hesed*:

O give thanks to the LORD, for he is good;
    his steadfast love [hesed] endures forever!"
                    (Psalm 118:1)

The LORD passed before him and proclaimed,

> *"The LORD, the LORD,*
> *a God merciful and gracious,*
> *slow to anger,*
> *and abounding in steadfast love [hesed] and faithfulness,*
> *keeping steadfast love [hesed] for the thousandth generation.*
>   *(Exodus 34:6-7a)*

This hesed isn't meant to be found only in God's posture toward humans, but also between humans.

This *hesed* isn't meant to be found only in God's posture toward humans, but also between humans. Experiencing God's faithful love is only the beginning. The goal is for *hesed* to be contagious, that as it is received the recipient is empowered and inspired to pass it along. The prophet Micah summed up God's requirements for human beings by boiling it all down to three things:

> *He has told you, O mortal, what is good,*
>   *and what does the LORD require of you*
> *but to do justice and to love kindness [hesed]*
>   *and to walk humbly with your God?*
>   *(Micah 6:8)*

On Shavuot, Israel embraced and entered into a relationship with the Divine that was based in mutual *hesed*. God would be loyal, faithful, and kind to Israel, and in turn, Israel would do the same toward God by practicing *hesed* toward their neighbor. This covenant, expressed in the Torah, is celebrated every Shavuot, and is central to the story of Ruth.

The character Ruth embodies *hesed* in many ways. While the word itself only appears three times in the book (1:8, 2:20, and 3:10), the idea and action of extending *hesed* permeates the story. As we will see, Ruth's commitment and loyalty to Naomi, summed up in her beautiful declaration in chapter one, verses sixteen and seventeen, is the focal point of the entire book, and it is tied to an audacious claim the author will make by the end. With all this in mind, we turn to the story of Ruth.

MOVING TO MOAB

The story of Ruth begins with a crisis for an Israelite family from Bethlehem. The curtain opens to reveal a food shortage, and a hard decision is made: they will become immigrants in another place in an attempt to survive: "In the days when the judges ruled, there was a famine in the land, and a certain man of Bethlehem in Judah went to live in the country of Moab, he and his wife and two sons" (Ruth 1:1).

Names are important in the Book of Ruth. Their meanings are tied to the story in significant ways. Take, for instance, the name *Ruth* itself. Ruth could mean "friend," which is very fitting for her character. However, another possible meaning for *Ruth* is "watering." In the context of a famine, and the events that will unfold that are so full of tragedy and loss, Ruth will emerge as an oasis in the desert. Another name, right at the beginning, is that of the town of *Bethlehem*.

In Hebrew *Bethlehem* means "house of bread." Ironically, as the story opens, we discover that, in the house of bread, there is no bread to be found. This family, made up of Elimelech, Naomi, and their two sons, Mahlon and Chilion, set off for Moab. I'd wager that Ruth's original audience would have had feelings about this decision that might be a little lost on us, so let's pause and look into their new, temporary home, Moab.

To call Israel and Moab enemies would be a significant understatement. Enshrined in the laws of Deuteronomy is a section about people who are excluded from participation in Israel (think in terms of marriage and Temple worship), and Moab was front and center. "No Ammonite or Moabite shall come into the assembly of the LORD even to the tenth generation. None of their descendants shall come into the assembly of the LORD forever" (Deuteronomy 23:3). This is a strong statement, amplified by the fact that it extends to "the tenth generation," a Hebrew idiom that essentially means "forever." Anyone from Moab would be a permanent outsider in Israel, according to Deuteronomy. This was a status that was irrevocable and unchangeable.

Yet, where do we find Elimelech, Naomi, and their sons? They are immigrants in Moab looking to provide a sustainable life for their family. It doesn't take long until they begin to put down roots. However, tragedy would soon strike the family as Elimelech died. Now, in a strange place among people she was taught to despise, Naomi and her sons must figure out how to exist. Mahlon and Chilion get married to two Moabite women, Orpah and Ruth. Things seemed to be looking up for this displaced family. But, as their names foreshadow, Mahlon (meaning "illness") and Chilion (meaning "destruction") soon meet the same fate as their father Elimelech: "When they had lived there about ten years, both Mahlon and Chilion also died, so that the woman was left without her two sons and her husband" (Ruth 1:4-5).

Naomi, now left with only her two daughters-in-law, must have felt such a mix of emotions. As women in a patriarchal society, all three of them were vulnerable as widows without the protection of a husband or father. Naomi was particularly vulnerable, being outside of her home in Israel, displaced and alone in a place that had been long considered an enemy of her people. When word reached her in Moab that God had given food—literally, bread—to the people back in Israel, she decided it was time to go home. Now that there was once again bread in the "house of bread," staying in Moab made little sense.

Naomi began the journey home with Ruth and Orpah alongside her. But it wasn't *their* home. It was then that Naomi gave the two women an out. She urges them to remain in Moab with their families of origin, or perhaps with a new husband. It was an emotional scene. Ruth and Orpah have done *hesed*, acted kindly, to Naomi and her sons, and now God will do the same to them—specifically in finding the security they all lack in the present moment. Ruth and Orpah resisted the idea that they would leave her, but Naomi became all the more insistent. The security she hoped for them—the house of a husband— she can never provide, because it would depend on Naomi having more sons. This is a reference to a practice called *levirate marriage*. According to Deuteronomy 25, when a man died without children, it was the responsibility of his brother to ensure that his name and legacy continued. This would be an impossibility for Ruth and Orpah, because as Naomi pointed out, would they just wait around for her to get married, have sons, and then marry them? It was a ridiculous proposition. At this, Orpah kissed Naomi and went back to her family of origin. Her name itself, *Orpah*, symbolizes this decision. It means "back of the neck," which would be visible to Naomi as Orpah turned and left. Ruth, however, would not be deterred. She "clung" to Naomi, which is the same word in Hebrew (*dâbaq*) that is used by the author of Genesis 2:24, "Therefore a man leaves his father and his mother and *clings* to his wife and they become one flesh" (emphasis mine). It implies a permanent bond. We might use the phrase "stuck like glue" to express the kind of commitment being implied with the word.

Naomi, one final time, tells Ruth to turn back, to return to her family of origin. Ruth responds with the words from Ruth 1:16-17 that began this chapter, words that reflect Ruth's commitment to not only remain with Naomi, but to also ensure her well-being. Once she realized that Ruth could not be persuaded to leave her, they, together, returned to Bethlehem.

When the two women arrived back in Bethlehem, it was obvious that Naomi was no longer the same person who had left all those years ago. Here, again, we discover the significance of names to the Book of Ruth. Naomi means "pleasant," but she could no longer live with the incongruity of her name and experience. She takes the name Mara, meaning "bitter," and she sees God as the source of her bitterness and emptiness. How many of us can relate to Naomi/Mara here? The weight and heaviness, complexity and grief of life come crashing in on us, often unexpectedly. There's a religious impulse to put on a mask, to pretend, to "fake it until you make it." That just won't work for Mara. She can't pretend that her world didn't come apart in Moab. She also can't pretend that she and God are on good terms about it all. Life is messy. Faith is messy. Mara reminds us that paying attention and feeling our experiences matters.

Chapter 1 ends with Naomi and Ruth together in Bethlehem. Notice the repetition of Moabite/Moab in this concluding verse. At almost every turn we will be reminded of who Ruth is (a Moabite) and from where she came (Moab). Try to hold in your mind all that we have learned about the relationship between Israel and Moab, as it will be the interpretive key that allows us to hear Ruth's message in its context.

HESED COMES FULL CIRCLE

In chapter 2 we are introduced to Boaz, whose name is of uncertain meaning, but might be connected to the idea of a "pillar." The name also shows up in 1 Kings 7:21 as the name of a pillar on the north side of the vestibule of the Jerusalem Temple. We immediately learn that Boaz was a significant figure in the community, and a relative of Naomi's deceased husband. It seems Boaz was also someone who followed the commands of the Torah. In order to ensure that the poor and vulnerable were cared for, Torah had built-in commands that called for generosity and consideration, like the following from Leviticus:

> *"When you reap the harvest of your land, you shall not reap to the very edges of your field or gather the gleanings of your harvest. You shall not strip your vineyard bare or gather the fallen grapes of your vineyard; you shall leave them for the poor and the alien: I am the LORD your God."*
>
> *(Leviticus 19:9-10)*

Boaz practiced this, and first encountered Ruth as she was gleaning behind the reapers in his field. He saw her and inquired about her. Notice, again, the repetition of Moabite/Moab in the response of Boaz's workers. "The young man who was in charge of the reapers answered,

"She is the young *Moabite* woman who came back with Naomi from the country of *Moab*" (Ruth 2:6, emphasis mine).

Ruth worked hard, trying to gather enough to sustain both herself and Naomi. Boaz invited her to remain in his field, he spoke kindly to her, offered her his protection, and a meal. Ruth was both grateful and surprised by his kindness, specifically because of her status as a foreigner. Boaz further instructed his workers to allow Ruth to glean as much as she wanted, and not just from the edges, but from that which had not yet been harvested as well. Boaz does this because he has heard about the way Ruth has treated Naomi. News of Ruth's *hesed* toward Naomi has spread, and it was being rewarded. Which is how *hesed* works. It's contagious, like when you're in line at a drive-through and somebody pays for your order, and then you pay for someone else's, and then…you get the picture.

The idea of someone being a redeemer *was that they would provide protection for vulnerable relatives.*

Ruth gleaned as much as she could—which was about five times more than they needed for that day. While they returned empty from Moab, Ruth's faithfulness inspired generosity that created abundance. Boaz's kindness sparked an idea for Naomi—she would play matchmaker between Boaz and Ruth. She concocted a plan for Ruth to seduce Boaz while he celebrated the barley harvest, which was accompanied by much eating and drinking. Ruth, however, abandoned the plan and challenged Boaz to do his duty as a "redeeming kinsman," *goel* in Hebrew. The idea of someone being a *redeemer* was that they would provide protection for vulnerable relatives. Here, Ruth calls Boaz to embrace his role. His response was effusive with praise for Ruth, and, of course, it's her loyalty (*hesed*) that inspired Boaz to grant her request.

There was one small snag, however. There was someone more closely related to Elimelech who would have to refuse the role of redeemer before Boaz could embrace it. Fortunately, he does refuse, and Boaz and Ruth are married. The happily ever after has begun. "So Boaz took Ruth, and she became his wife. When they came together, the LORD made her conceive, and she bore a son…They named him Obed; he became the father of Jesse, the father of David" (Ruth 4:13, 17b).

The line of Elimelech, which seemed to be at an end, has been restored and continued. Ruth and Boaz have given Naomi a son (remember the idea of levirate marriage) to perpetuate the family line—and what a lineage that would become. Let this sink in for just a moment. Ruth the Moabite, as we've been reminded again and again, is the great-grandmother of David, who would become Israel's greatest king. Assuming you'd never read or heard this story before, this would be kind of shocking, right? Especially with all that we know about Moabites—they are permanently excluded from Israel. Yet, here, we have a Moabite woman in the genealogy of king David. Hopefully all the alarms, bells, and whistles are sounding for you right now. Before we draw some conclusions about what this means, let's pause to talk about the setting in which Ruth was written.

THE WHEN OF RUTH

The opening lines of the book tell us the setting of the story of Ruth: "In the days when the judges ruled…" That is a particular time between the entrance into/conquest of the land Canaan and the beginning of the monarchy in Israel, roughly the period between 1200 and 1000 BCE. However, that opening line, "In the days when the judges ruled…" has a certain quality to it that sounds familiar to me. It seems akin to "Once upon a time," or "A long time ago, in a galaxy far, far away." It's setting the story in a particular time and place, but is it possible it's actually being written about a different time and place? I think so.

Both the language and style of Ruth cause many scholars to argue for a date of composition after the return from Exile in 5th century BCE. Briefly, after the time of Solomon, David's son, the United Kingdom was torn in two by civil war. The Northern Kingdom, Israel, broke away from what became the Southern Kingdom of Judah. Eventually both kingdoms would be gobbled up by the powerful empires of their day. Israel would cease to exist in the year 722 BCE when the Assyrians conquered and exiled the kingdom. Though they survived Assyrian dominance, Judah would eventually be destroyed and exiled by Babylon in 587/6 BCE. However, Babylon would not remain in power long. They would be conquered themselves by Cyrus the Great of Persia in the year 539 BCE. While Babylon enacted a policy of deportation of conquered peoples, the Persian Empire operated under a different approach. In 538 BCE, Cyrus issued a decree allowing the Jews to return home to their land and to rebuild their Temple (Ezra 1). This period of return from Exile is the "when" that the Book of Ruth was likely written, and the book itself is a response to what was happening in this era of returning and rebuilding. Two of the central figures from this time period were Ezra and Nehemiah. As we have already seen, their books are part of the *Ketuvim*, the "Writings" section of the Hebrew Bible, and they describe this not only as a time of returning and rebuilding physically, but a similar experience was happening within the community itself. While they had survived the destruction of Jerusalem and the Exile in Babylon as a community, their siblings to the north in Israel had not. Why did they experience destruction and exile? Though they had survived this time, how could they ensure their longevity as a people, and avoid being absorbed into the broader cultures that surrounded and always threatened them?

The consensus of scholars is that it was also in this same period that what we know as the Torah—the first five books of the Hebrew Bible—was completed and began to be read. From the perspective of many of the Jews returning home from exile, the only thing that stood between them and absorption (at best) and annihilation (at worst) was faithfulness to the Torah. So, when Ezra read from the Torah to the people, they realized they were not living faithfully within the covenant boundaries, especially in terms of marriage, and this unfaithfulness was the cause of their suffering in the past and could lead to more trouble in the future.

> After these things had been done, the officials approached me and said,
> "The people of Israel, the priests, and the Levites have not separated
> themselves from the peoples of the lands with their abominations, from
> the Canaanites, the Hittites, the Perizzites, the Jebusites, the Ammonites,
> the Moabites, the Egyptians, and the Amorites. For they have taken some
> of their daughters as wives for themselves and for their sons. Thus the holy
> seed has mixed itself with the peoples of the lands, and in this faithlessness
> the officials and leaders have led the way."
>
> Ezra 9:1-2

Ezra, after a time of mourning and prayer, announced the solution to the problem of intermarriage: "Then Ezra the priest stood up and said to them, 'You have trespassed and married foreign women and so increased the guilt of Israel. Now make confession to the LORD the God of your ancestors and do his will; separate yourselves from the peoples of the land and from the foreign wives'" (Ezra 10:10-11).

It's important to understand the full weight of the pronouncement being made and the reforms being enacted. Moabites could never, ever, ever "enter the assembly of God" (Nehemiah 13:1). Which means that they could never be part of the community—specifically, they couldn't marry into the community or worship at the Temple.

Into this setting comes the Book of Ruth, telling a story of hero-ism and *hesed*, all centered upon a woman that we are reminded, again and again, is from Moab. If Ruth lived during the reforms of Ezra, she would be sent away, back home to Moab, with her son, Obed. David would have likely never been born, in the scenario.

The context of Ruth's story completely transforms its meaning. Through this lens, Ruth is not simply an idyll tale or a love story, but a resistance to—or protest against—the Ezra-Nehemiah reforms. The point isn't just that Ruth embodied *hesed* in her commitment to Naomi (expressed in the beautiful poetry of Ruth 1:16-17), but that Ruth, the MOABITE, embodied *hesed* to Naomi, the Israelite. This is why we are reminded again and again throughout the course of this small book that Ruth was a Moabite from Moab, lest we get to the end and miss the entire point: God had worked in Israel's favor and interest in the past using unexpected people. To suggest Ruth did not belong, or that she should have been sent away, would be directly opposed to God's action, because it is God who enables Ruth to conceive. And, if Ruth the Moabite is removed from the family tree, then David, Solomon, and the entire monarchy are lost, never to be born. Who might be removed in the future if the reforms of Ezra and Nehemiah are carried to the extreme? This unknown author has constructed quite the case, and offers it in the context of a lovely, and surprisingly challenging, story.

IT'S A LOVE STORY AFTER ALL

Before we continue, a confession. I love *love*. If left to my own devices I will choose a romantic comedy almost every time. It's probably no surprise, then, that one of my favorite parts of my job as a pastor is to perform weddings. Having a front row seat to all the excitement and emotions experienced on that day is pretty lovely. It makes sense why people would want to include our passage (Ruth 1:16-17) in their wedding ceremonies. The words reflect a dedication and commitment that feels similar to the kind being expressed in a marriage. Ruth is, after all, a love story; it just isn't about romantic love. Remember, these words are spoken between a young widow and her mother-in-law. Ruth could have just stayed at home in Moab with her family of origin. Instead, she, like the woman unearthed holding the child in Lajia, provided for and protected Naomi not because she had to, but because she embodied *hesed*. As a result, she transformed the future of Israel, and the world, forever. That is what *hesed* does. It gives and pours itself out without having personal interest at stake. This is what makes Ruth such a profound text, and one of my favorite stories in all the Bible, that this kind of commitment is being expressed by someone considered to be an unwelcome outsider who has no reason to do so. This is why the context for this passage is so important, because to miss it is to also miss the powerful example Ruth becomes of God's *hesed* being discovered in unexpected places and experienced from surprising sources.

THE INVITATION OF RUTH

As we conclude this chapter, I want to offer some takeaways that might help us think through what the significance the Book of Ruth has today. First, Ruth is set in the time of the Judges, as we've seen. In fact, four times the Book of Judges tells us that this was a time in Israel where leadership was greatly lacking: "In those days there was no king in Israel; all the people did what was right in their own eyes" (Judges 17:6, 18:1, 19:1, 21:25).

It is in this period that Ruth is set, and she provides leadership in ways that shape, not only her and Naomi's fate, but the destiny of Israel. She steps in at a critical time and ensures the stability and future of a people who were not hers by birth but became hers through her actions. Ruth's enacting of *hesed* was more powerful than the boundaries and barriers that were set up to keep her out. Perhaps that is what *hesed* is meant to do—it is a loving-kindness so powerful that it has the capacity to heal, transform, and create new realities.

Another important takeaway is that Ruth is asking us, even today, to make space for surprises. Throughout Scripture we find our spiritual ancestors having their assumptions about people—individuals and entire groups—challenged. It happened when God called Jonah to go to Nineveh, and again when Elisha healed Naaman, the Syrian. It also happened with a Moabite woman named Ruth. Her story, if we are willing to hear and embrace its challenge, will call us beyond our comfort and isolation, but it will also open up new and exciting possibilities to experience the beauty of God and others.

Isn't it a little surprising that both Ruth and Ezra-Nehemiah are in the canon of Scripture and even, within the Hebrew Bible, in the same section? This is an example of the conversations that are found within the Bible that I mentioned in the introduction. These are two differing understandings, two different perspectives, and they both live together within the library we call Scripture as a reminder to us that our faith traditions aren't meant to be monologues but dialogues. The tension, debate, and disagreement are signs of life, of people trying to sort out the way forward. The Bible itself gives us permission—no, more than that—it gives us an invitation to wrestle with these texts, enter into these conversations, and make decisions about which voices are leading us toward human flourishing for all people.

Fear never inspires us to be our best selves.

The Book of Ruth is especially significant in the context of America in the twenty-first century. It would be an understatement to say that the surge of xenophobia and nationalism we have experienced in recent years has been alarming. Especially troublesome is how religion—specifically Christianity—has been used to support and defend such exclusionary perspectives. The track record of our faith tradition and nationalism is one of human history's ugliest examples of what can happen when human beings allow fear to become their compass. Fear never inspires us to be our best selves. It doesn't expand our creativity. Far from it, fear causes us most often to tap into our worst impulses. The Book of Ruth offers a gentle, yet firm, challenge to all forms of nationalism and xenophobia, calling us to make benevolent space for the "other," whomever that may be for us.

45

Ruth 1:16-17, in context, sums up the meaning of this short, provocative, and beautiful story. Ruth's enacting of *hesed* toward Naomi—Ruth the *Moabite*, mind you—becomes a central, pivotal moment in the history of Judaism. If we pay attention, this story can create awareness, challenge, and shape how we show up in the world around us. If we are people who practice *hesed*, how might the lives and futures around us (even our own) become transformed? That is the invitation with which Ruth leaves us.

CHAPTER 3

"You Always Have the Poor with You"

Mark 14:7

CHAPTER 3

"You Always Have the Poor with You"

(Mark 14:7)

The Bible has been an ever-present part of my life. Before I was able to read, I was already memorizing passages of Scripture (full disclosure, it wasn't as much out of piety as it was to win prizes in what we called "Sword Drills"). It wasn't until my early twenties that I began really to engage the Bible thoughtfully, however. By thoughtfully I mean beyond the main stories and beyond surface meanings or the interpretations that I'd been handed. In my twenties, I fell in love with the Bible.

It was that taking seriously and falling in love with the Bible that presented me with a conundrum. As I read the Bible from cover to cover, I noticed a consistent message, and it was one I had never really heard talked about in church growing up. That message is that God cares about justice. Specifically, God cares about the poor, the oppressed, and the marginalized. We didn't spend much time on that idea in my churches. We focused on what we needed to believe about

49

God, Jesus, and the Bible in order to be saved, which meant going to heaven when we die. This emphasis on God's care for the people that have been rejected or forgotten by society was new for me. Sure, Jesus regularly pulled people in from the edges, but that was about saving their soul, not caring for their physical needs, right?

Once I became aware of this theme, in both halves of the Bible, I couldn't unsee it. I started preaching more from the Prophets and Jesus's words about God's justice. To my surprise it made many people in my congregation uncomfortable. I was starting to preach a "social gospel," they said, "and Jesus came to save our souls, not transform society."

When I was met with this criticism it was complete with a proof text, straight from the lips of Jesus himself. In Mark 14, Jesus's disciples are angry about an unnamed woman who uses a jar of expensive ointment to anoint Jesus's head in an act of extravagant love and devotion. Their frustration is grounded in what they called the wasting of resources. The ointment could have been sold and the proceeds given to the poor, they insist. Jesus responds with what, on the surface, seems to be a cold and uncaring response in her defense.

Was Jesus really advocating that some people experiencing poverty was a divine necessity?

He tells them not to trouble her, because "you always have the poor with you, and you can show kindness to them whenever you wish…" (Mark 14:7). This is the passage that I would hear referenced time and time again in response to preaching and teaching about God's concern for the poor. The standard interpretation was taken to be that, if we end poverty and no one is poor, then Jesus would be wrong, because he said that there would always be some who are poor in the world. It must just be the way God designed it, was the conclusion, because Jesus can't be wrong. The first time that verse was quoted to me I was stunned. Surely Jesus never said such a thing. Yet, when I turned to Mark 14:7, there it was in black, white, and red. Was Jesus really advocating that some people experiencing poverty was a divine necessity? Would God really be disappointed, or worse, angry, with us if we created a world of justice and equity? I could not fathom that being the case. If we place these words back into their context in Mark, is it possible that something else is happening? Before we do just that, let's think about the larger context of the Gospel according to Mark.

MY GOSPEL CRUSH

Cards on the table: I love the Gospel of Mark. It's my Gospel crush, the one I feel most drawn to and reference most often. That's why I chose Mark's account of this story, instead of the parallel versions in Matthew 26 and John 12 (Luke reports a different anointing story that occurs earlier in his narrative). But why do I love Mark so much?

Mark is my favorite partly because it was the first of our New Testament Gospels to be written. A brief explanation of the timeline of the New Testament writings might be helpful here. In terms of the twenty-seven books that make up the New Testament, the earliest writings we have are the seven undisputed letters of Paul. If this language is new to you, it just refers to the scholarly consensus that, based on language and content, we can be confident that Paul wrote at least seven of the thirteen letters attributed to him (1 Thessalonians, Galatians, 1 and 2 Corinthians, Philippians, Philemon, and Romans). The other six letters contain themes and contexts that scholars see reflecting a time period after Paul's death in the mid 60s CE. That means the earliest documents in the New Testament were written in the 50s, or between twenty and thirty years after Jesus lived.

After Paul, Mark is next in line. Scholars date Mark at or near the year 70 CE, which was a cataclysmic time for the occupants of what Rome called "Judea." In 66 CE, amid decades-long and growing tensions related to taxation and the expanding gap between the wealthy and the poor, the Jews in Judea rebelled against Roman rule. The conflict was violent and intense. While the war proper would last until 73 CE, it was in 70 CE that Rome destroyed Jerusalem and the Second Jewish Temple. According to tradition, the Second Temple was razed on the same day the Babylonians had demolished the First, only roughly six hundred years later, on Tisha B'Av, a date that falls in July or August depending on the year. The event that is described in Mark 13 is seen as the end of the age, and its impact on life for Jews in Judea, including the early followers of Jesus, can't be over emphasized. As the earliest Gospel to be written, Mark is telling the Jesus story at the end of one age and the beginning of another. Mark wonders, what if Jesus's message and method (the nonviolent kingdom of God) had been embraced?

I am probably drawn to Mark, in part, because it is the shortest Gospel, which means it moves with a certain urgency and action in telling the Jesus story. Being the first also means that it serves as our literary introduction to Jesus and the cast of characters that would play a central role in the story of his life and death, as well as the early movement that continued in response to the Easter experience. The other Gospels came later and at least Matthew and Luke used Mark as a significant source for their own narrative. Matthew wrote in the 80s and used 90 percent of Mark, incorporating 600 of Mark's 678 verses. Luke, dated between the late 80s and early 100s, used 65 percent of Mark. In the 90s John seems to be doing his own thing, but there are scholars who argue that the writer of John was in fact aware of Mark. Mark, we could say, was a trendsetter.

Another feature of Mark's approach is the use of specific techniques and themes, two of which will be important for our study of this text in particular. One such technique is commonly called the "Markan Sandwich" (although the technical term is *intercalation*). Practically, this refers to a motif of Mark that divides a story into two by sandwiching a second story in between, following an A - B - A pattern. The sandwiched story isn't just for style points but serves to interpret the surrounding story. For example, in Mark 5, Jesus was going to the house of Jairus, a synagogue leader, to heal his twelve-year old daughter. The opening encounter between Jesus and Jairus is interrupted by a large crowd and the healing of a woman who had suffered from bleeding for twelve years. Finally, the focus of the story shifts back to Jairus's daughter's healing. These "Markan Sandwiches" occur nine times throughout the Gospel, including the story at which we are looking.

Our main focus is the B section of the intercalation, the story of Jesus being anointed by an unnamed woman with a very expensive ointment (Mark 14:3-9), but that story is sandwiched by another narrative. The sandwich looks like this:

A: The plot to arrest and kill Jesus (vv. 11-2)
B: The anointing at Bethany (vv. 3-9)
A: Judas volunteers to be the betrayer (vv. 10-11)

Now we turn to a central theme of Mark: failed discipleship. Again and again Jesus's closest friends and followers seem to misunderstand or do not grasp his mission. This isn't an isolated failure, but one that permeates the entirety of the Gospel's story. From the disciples' collective inability to cast out an unclean spirit, to Peter's rebuke of Jesus's insistence that he will die, and climaxing in the disciples' abandonment of Jesus at his arrest, trial, and execution, Mark does not spare them critique. Mark resists the urge we have to dress someone up a little more after their death, our tendency to remember them, perhaps, a little more generously by minimizing their flaws and failures. Not Mark. He puts on unvarnished display the flaws and failures of Jesus's inner circle, who, by the way, would go on to lead his movement. It makes me wonder, how would those who knew Peter, James, John, and the others have received Mark's version of them?

Setting Mark within the world of the writer and paying close attention to the techniques and themes isn't just an exercise for those of us who identify as "Bible nerds." In the case of our story in Mark 14, it is central to understanding the meaning Mark is embedding in this episode. Try to keep this context in the back of your mind as we move forward, as it will inform where we go with this passage.

THE ANOINTING AT BETHANY

It's Wednesday. We are smack dab in the middle of that liturgical time Christians call *Holy Week*, the final week of Jesus's life, and the tension around Jesus's message is growing more palpable by the day. Up until this point in Mark, Jesus's ministry was confined to the rural communities of Galilee, the northern region that he called home.

Eventually, he decided to take the message to Jerusalem, the center of religious, political, and economic life. Though his ministry had been based in Galilee, in the North, Jesus did have connections down South, and it seems he used the town of Bethany as a kind of home base or staging ground. This is evidenced by his rhythm during Holy Week: He would go into the city and engage in prophetic action or teaching, and then, when the temperature rose too high, he would leave the city and regroup in Bethany, less than two miles away. It was there, in the safety of his friends, that an unnamed woman would offer an extravagant and generous gesture that makes her, according to Jesus, a model disciple—much to the chagrin of the others.

The story begins in the home of Simon who is identified as a "leper," a term that indicates some sort of skin disease that would have caused anyone afflicted to be kept isolated and at a distance (see Leviticus 13). We don't know anything about this Simon who plays host for Jesus. Was he currently dealing with his disease? Had he dealt with it in the past, but was now cured? We have no way of knowing. However, what we know about Jesus means that his presence in Simon's home is not a surprise to us. Being in that space was a very Jesus thing to do.

Normally a meal with Jesus would be a celebratory environment, enacting the Kingdom in real time by sharing the basic necessities of life.

I imagine a scene that is different than Jesus's usual meals. Normally a meal with Jesus would be a celebratory environment, enacting the

Kingdom in real time by sharing the basic necessities of life—all gifts from God—of food and drink. But this meal is different. The vibe during this week had changed, from the jubilation of Palm Sunday to, now, a rising concern among Jesus's followers. The Kingdom hadn't just appeared like they'd expected. In fact, Jesus has been met with fierce opposition from those in power. His Kingdom message was causing a stir during an already tense season.

Passover was a time when the city of Jerusalem would be bursting with pilgrims who had made the journey to the Holy City for the festival. It was also a time of heightened awareness that living under Roman rule was in conflict with the very theme of the season, that God wills the liberation of God's people. Jesus choosing this particular time to make his journey to Jerusalem was strategic, and very dangerous. His provocations during this week were the equivalent of living in a powder keg and giving off sparks.

Imagine with me a room that is tense, and perhaps there are voices growing loud with passion as they debate what the next move should be. One suggests they lie low and let the dust settle, while another calls them to ramp up the pressure and provocation. Suddenly, a woman enters. She's unnoticed at first, that is until the room is hushed to silence as she breaks open an expensive jar of perfume and pours it on Jesus's head.

Mark's readers would have immediately understood the significance of such an event. Someone being anointed in this way was full of meaning, all of which would have been controversial in this setting. After all, *Christ* is not Jesus's last name, but a title. It is the Greek rendering of a Hebrew word that gives us *Messiah* in English. The literal translation is "Anointed One." This unnamed woman is making a bold claim about Jesus through this extravagant act. She also is stepping into a role usually reserved for a prophet, because it was the responsibility of a prophet to anoint the person who would become the next king of Israel. By anointing Jesus this woman takes up the mantle of a prophet who has been given insight from God to understand who Jesus was.

The disciples were stunned, and they immediately began to criticize the woman's action.

> But some were there who said to one another in anger, "Why was the ointment wasted in this way? For this ointment could have been sold for more than three hundred denarii and the money given to the poor." And they scolded her.
>
> (Mark 14:4-5)

John's version of the story names names. It was Judas Iscariot who questioned the woman's action, but not because he cared for the poor, John tells us. It was because "he was a thief; he kept the common purse and used to steal what was put into it" (John 12:6). Mark doesn't go that far, instead indicating this was the consensus among some angry disciples.

Their frustration was couched as concern for the poor. Surely it would have been a better decision to sell the perfume. To put the value of the ointment into perspective, a denarius was a day's wage for a day laborer. That means the disciples estimate that this ointment, which would have come from the Himalayan region, would be worth over three hundred day's wages. That's some pricey perfume, to say the least, and she's just wasted it. Getting lost in the mix is this woman. She's a person, after all, and she is now on the receiving end of shame and ridicule. She must have felt embarrassed.

Jesus responded to the accusation of "waste" by calling the disciples' focus back onto the woman and her lavish action. She isn't to be corrected, Jesus says, but celebrated. In his response to their protestation about the perfume being sold and the money given to the poor, the central verse we are contextualizing in this chapter occurs.

> *But Jesus said, "Let her alone; why do you trouble her? She has performed a good service for me. For you always have the poor with you, and you can show kindness to them whenever you wish, but you will not always have me. She has done what she could; she has anointed my body beforehand for its burial. Truly I tell you, wherever the good news is proclaimed in the whole world, what she has done will be told in remembrance of her."*
>
> (Mark 14:6-9)

Anointing was traditionally a moment of triumph. A new king ascending to the throne was a moment to be celebrated. This anointing, however, was not a celebration but a preparation for burial. This woman preemptively cares for Jesus's body, affording him the dignity he will be denied in death. Her act was a gift, and a recognition of not only who Jesus was as Messiah, but also the kind of messiah he would be. Jesus would not be a conqueror or employ violence. Instead, Jesus would be the victim of the empire's brutality.

YOU WILL ALWAYS HAVE THE POOR

Jesus's answer to the disciples' suggestion that the ointment be sold and the proceeds given to the poor isn't original to Jesus. The first line is a quotation from the Book of Deuteronomy, chapter 15. This chapter contains laws that focus on the Sabbath Year, which meant among other things that every seventh year there would be a remission of debts in Israel. Anyone who owed someone else a debt would have that debt forgiven. The Sabbath Year was a kind of mini-Jubilee, which was an even larger societal economic reset, during which anyone who had sold or lost their family land to indebtedness would receive it back.

The purpose of such provisions was to ensure that, if followed, the gap between the rich and the poor would not expand unchecked, and that there would not always be endless poverty. However, if not followed, there would always be some who are poor, and the command was to care for them generously. This is the context of the verse Jesus quotes in Mark 14: "Since there will never cease to be some in need on the earth, I therefore command you, 'Open your hand to the poor and needy neighbor in your land'" (Deuteronomy 15:11).

Notice that this is not a command that there will always be someone in need, but an acknowledgment that such people exist. The command that follows is a call to be generous with those in need. It's not a Divine decree that poverty exist, but a Divine mandate to provide care for those who are struggling.

THE OUTSIDE OF THE SANDWICH

Setting the reference in context is only the first step. Why would Jesus quote this text here? How does it make sense in this situation with his disciples' critique of this woman's act of devotion? This is where the story Mark uses to frame this encounter comes into focus. Let's explore the outside of the sandwich.

If you'll recall, Mark uses an A-B-A approach to framing stories. For the story of the woman who anoints Jesus, the framing story involves a plot to arrest and kill Jesus. It begins with the Passover nearing, and the chief priests trying to find a stealthy way to make their Jesus problem go away. Before we continue it's important to pause here and acknowledge the tragic ways the Jesus story has been used as a smokescreen for antisemitism. Passages like this have been used to place the blame for Jesus's death onto Jewish people. This is wrong and couldn't be further from the truth. Rome killed Jesus, and only Rome had the authority to do so. The reality is that Jesus was popular among the crowds of pilgrims in Jerusalem. He was celebrated as a liberator of the people on Palm Sunday as he entered the city. Jesus did clash with the Temple authorities. They had very different visions.

In his critique of the Temple, Jesus channels the words of the prophet Jeremiah who lived at a similar time when another powerful empire (Babylon) was looming as a threat. Jesus saw the Temple leaders as being in collaboration with Rome, and thus making the Temple a "den of robbers," instead of a "house of prayer" (Mark 11:17). Rome would often use indigenous institutions as client rulers, and if you want to keep the populace in check, finding ways to partner with the institutions that held influence over them was the way to do it. There is no doubt in my mind that Jesus was frustrated by the Temple leadership, and they didn't care for his message either. However, that historical reality is an inter-family disagreement. Jesus was Jewish, and so were the Temple authorities. Their argument was not about a new religion, Christianity, versus Judaism, but what it meant to be faithfully Jewish.

So, the sandwich begins with a plot that is beginning to develop to get rid of Jesus. The second framing story is the solution to the first. After the woman anoints Jesus and he celebrates her as the example of faithful discipleship ("wherever the good news is proclaimed in the whole world, what she has done will be told in remembrance of her" [Mark 14:9]), Judas, a member of Jesus's inner circle, goes to the authorities and agrees to betray Jesus in exchange for payment.

If we hold these two characters side by side, Judas and the unnamed woman, we discover glaring contradictions between them. This woman carries out her action publicly and gives a generous gift to Jesus. On the contrary, Judas acts in secrecy and enriches himself at Jesus's expense. In that light, the two are exact opposites of one another.

What does this story of Jesus being anointed by an unnamed woman have to do with the surrounding story about the plot against Jesus that is beginning to unfold?

CHARITY OR JUSTICE?

Jesus's quotation of Deuteronomy 15 is accompanied by a statement that is meant to critique the attitude of his disciples. "For you always have the poor with you," Jesus says, "and you can show kindness to them whenever you wish" (Mark 14:7). Jesus pushes back on his disciples' critique, not by saying the poor don't matter or discouraging care for them. Instead, he is getting at the core of his Kingdom vision, which was grounded in justice and jubilee. When Jesus quoted this text, his disciples would very likely have understood the larger context of Deuteronomy 15, that it was not a command to enact charity, but a command to practice justice. Those are two different things, charity and justice.

Charity is a band-aid solution to the problem of poverty. It helps a person or group of people in the moment, which is wonderful, but it fails to address the root causes of the problem. That's exactly what Deuteronomy 15 is addressing, getting to the roots of poverty and ensuring that the poor will not always be with us, because the systems and structures that create poverty have been dismantled and addressed.

On April 4, 1967, exactly one year to the day before he would be murdered, Martin Luther King Jr. gave a sermon called "Beyond

Vietnam: A Time to Break Silence" at the Riverside Church in New York that was critical of the Vietnam War. Dr. King took a great deal of criticism on all sides as a result. Toward the end of the speech King summed up exactly what Jesus is speaking to in Mark 14: "True compassion is more than flinging a coin to a beggar; it is not haphazard and superficial. It comes to see that an edifice which produces beggars needs restructuring."

Jesus's message and movement were centered on the least, the forgotten, the excluded, the oppressed, and the marginalized.

Jesus's message and movement were centered on the least, the forgotten, the excluded, the oppressed, and the marginalized. He is not discouraging his disciples, then or now, from caring about the poor. So far from it. He is calling his disciples, then and now, to do more than random acts of charity, but instead to transform the systems that create poverty for some in the first place. Jesus's reference to Deuteronomy 15 is not a call to do less for the poor; it's a call to do more, to transform unjust systems into something just and equitable.

Since this perspective on Jesus's message might be different for many of us, let me offer one example of how Jesus engages in this call for systemic transformation. In Mark 12, a day earlier than the story we've been examining in Mark 14, Jesus and his disciples were sitting near the Temple treasury watching the crowd giving their money. He noticed a poor widow who came and gave two small coins, which in today's market would be worth less than a penny. Yet, it was all she had on which to live. Jesus called his disciples' attention to her and told them that she had given far more than the others who gave out of their abundance, because she had given everything she had.

Often this story is used by preachers to encourage their church members to give sacrificially to the church offering. However, I don't think that's what Jesus is doing here. A few verses before this encounter Jesus warns his disciples against those who "devour widows' houses" (12:40). The pronouncement here isn't celebrating the widow who gave all she had, but critiquing and challenging a system that would take her last two coins. Both here and in Mark 14, Jesus isn't ensuring that the poor will always exist. He's calling for a transformation of the structures and systems that create poverty. As we know all too well, you're taking your life into your hands if you start talking to people about their money. Jesus's experience would be no different.

A FAILURE OF DISCIPLESHIP

As mentioned earlier, one of Mark's central themes is the failure of Jesus's disciples. It would seem to be a historically reliable detail, otherwise why would Mark include it? Why would he risk undermining the leaders who took over the movement after Jesus's death unless it was a well-known fact that those closest to Jesus had failed him in such ways? The historical reality is likely that those who knew Jesus best and followed him most closely were also those who regularly just didn't understand what he was up to (and I, for one, find a little comfort in that).

We can sum up the failures of the disciples throughout Mark's narrative as a *failure of imagination*. At the core, the problem for them is that they just cannot imagine the world Jesus is proclaiming and creating actually being a possibility. The issues were too big. They were too small, too few. Rome was too powerful. So, when Jesus told enigmatic stories about an upside down, counterintuitive Kingdom that wasn't somewhere else, but right here and available right now, they couldn't totally understand how. When large crowds followed them into the wilderness and needed food, they thought it was an impossible task to provide a meal. Even when Peter rightly identifies Jesus as the Christ, only a few verses later he then rebukes Jesus for saying that he would suffer and die at the hands of the authorities. The most jarring moment came when Jesus was betrayed by one of them, all the rest abandoned him, and Peter denied him. They just couldn't fully trust that the world Jesus was seeking to create was a possibility in the context of Roman occupation.

Yet, this unnamed woman becomes, for Jesus, the model disciple who does have the capacity for imagination. Isn't it interesting that it is right after her anointing of Jesus, and his celebration of her, that Judas decided to betray Jesus? What was it about this moment that flipped the switch for him? Could it be that this moment was the first time Judas really understood Jesus's message and that it was not the revolution he thought he was joining? How could Jesus really bring the Kingdom when he rejected violence and would himself suffer it? Did Judas hope to force Jesus's hand? Did he expect Jesus to change his mind when Roman soldiers were surrounding him? Or did Judas decide that Jesus's approach was weak and ineffective?

This unnamed woman will be remembered differently. She understood that Jesus would be broken and poured, just like her jar of ointment, so she prepared him for burial in advance. It was an act of kindness, compassion, human dignity, courage, and faith. By anointing Jesus, she shows the capacity to imagine the different kind of world that he announced, and that his suffering would not be the end of that vision.

THE CONNECTION COMES INTO FOCUS

If you recall earlier we said that in the A-B-A format of the Markan Sandwich, the B "filling" is designed to help us interpret the outer layers. What does the action of this woman have to do with the plot to arrest and execute Jesus? Simply put, it is her action that reveals the disjointedness between Jesus's and Judas's ideas about the *how*. They were in agreement about the *what*: The coming of the Kingdom, the removal of the oppressors, the need for drastic societal change, and liberation for Israel. The major rift that was exposed by the woman's action, and Jesus's celebration of it, was that Judas could not, would not, accept Jesus's methods for getting it done.

Judas is the ultimate example of failed discipleship. He lacks the imagination and vision to see what Jesus is doing. Instead of embracing Jesus's program of resistance through nonviolence, Judas betrays him to those who would enact violence against him. This is a pointed message for Mark, writing in the aftermath of the destruction of Jerusalem and the Temple in the year 70 CE. He's using this contrast between Judas and the woman to reflect on the choice to rebel violently against Rome. As Jesus warns in Mark 13:2, "Not one stone will be left here upon another; all will be thrown down." Mark's first readers would have understood the very real implications of the choice Judas represented.

65

The woman, however, embodies the opposite. She is an example of faithful discipleship for Mark, of someone who understood Jesus's message and methods and trusted his vision for what the world could become. Her story's inclusion in the overarching narrative about a plot and a betrayer cause Judas's failure to embrace Jesus's message to be all the more shocking for us. Her faithfulness trust, and generosity, side by side with Judas's offer to join the plot against Jesus, are a stark contrast.

MAKING CHANGE REAL

Taking a random line of Scripture out of context and then using it to argue against caring for the poor requires little creative effort, and it does a lot of harm. But digging deeper, as we've done here, and discovering the larger background in which this text is found, offers us a different perspective, one that resonates with the rest of Jesus's teaching and ministry. If we are willing to do the difficult work, if we will collaborate with the Spirit who is always leading us toward justice, then we can transform the world into a place in which everyone has enough.

As we've seen, Jesus's quotation of Deuteronomy 15 was an invitation to his disciples to join him in imagining a more just world in which there was no poverty. A world that could be made real, not through violence, but through embracing the vision of the Sabbath Year/Jubilee. We've also borne witness to two different responses to that invitation. Judas and this unnamed woman are our archetypes. All these years later we are left to decide which person's action we will imitate.

A real transformation of the world into a just and generous place, in which everyone has enough, is still a daunting task. We feel so far away from the kind of world the prophets dreamed about, a world in which everyone "shall all sit under their own vines and under their own fig trees, and no one shall make them afraid…" (Micah 4:4). Enough to eat, shelter, and not fear. That is the possibility held out for our future by the Hebrew Prophets, including Jesus.

A real transformation of the world into a just and generous place, in which everyone has enough, is still a daunting task.

If we want to take Jesus seriously today, that means grappling with the difficult questions that his message evokes: How will we use our resources individually and collectively? Are we willing to be inconvenienced personally to see real change societally? Do we believe it can happen, that the world become a just and equitable place? Could we really cultivate that kind of reality? Not unless we can imagine it, and not unless we are willing to act courageously and generously, just like this woman. It seems that Jesus was right about her because we are still telling her story today, and she is still remembered as an example of faithful discipleship.

Change begins in the imagination and enters the real world when we decide to act. Making change real requires our participation. May we, like this woman, unnamed and yet celebrated wherever good news is announced, understand the challenge and vision of Jesus, and may we use our energy, creativity, and courage to make it so.

CHAPTER 4

"For Surely I Know the Plans I Have for You"

Jeremiah 29:11

CHAPTER 4

"For Surely I Know the Plans I Have for You"
(Jeremiah 29:11)

My first job on a church staff came at the ripe old age of nineteen. I was hired as the interim pastor of my home church, the First Baptist Church of Belfry, Kentucky. I don't know what either of us were thinking, but that opportunity at such a young age was extraordinarily helpful and meaningful.

Recently I stumbled upon a church bulletin from my final Sunday in the interim role, and I noticed my mom had made notes about the final sermon I had given. Apparently, I had shared a few of my (at the time) favorite scriptures with the congregation, leaving them a parting encouragement based on a collage of our context references, which is exactly the opposite of what I hope to do in this book. Oh, the irony. The saying is true, "When you know better, you do better."

One of the scriptures I shared on that final day was from the Book of Jeremiah. Back then I would have quoted it from the NIV: "For I know the plans I have for you," declares the LORD, "plans to prosper you and not to harm you, plans to give you hope and a future" (29:11).

I had not arrived at this verse as a favorite in a vacuum. This verse was regularly quoted and shared in our youth group. It was even printed on a poster that adorned the wall, reminding us that God had a plan for our lives, and it was up to us to be obedient if we wanted to discover that plan. Failure to do so could lead to missing out on what God had intended for our lives, and if that were to happen then the entirety of our existence moving forward would be diminished. Our lives would be significantly less than they could have been. That was a lot of pressure for our teenaged selves to process. I was keenly aware at, say, sixteen years old, that God's plan for me was good, but if I wavered in my faith, it might not come to pass. What if I married the wrong person? took the wrong job? went to the wrong college? The what-ifs led to lots of sleepless nights, wondering how my actions might impact God's specific, individual-for-me plan.

It was years later that I realized that the Book of Jeremiah was not just a collection of random verses meant to be lifted here and there to construct a theology, but it was instead a collection of the words and actions of a prophet that, in many ways, could be and has been considered a failure throughout the generations since his time. But, that is getting ahead of ourselves. What has become evident to me is that the use of Jeremiah 29:11, divorced from its context, can be seriously harmful to many people. Let's begin by setting the verse in its larger context, and then we can begin to see why it might be so potentially harmful when it is quoted without that context in view.

MARCHING TOWARD EXILE

Jeremiah's work spanned the reigns of three Judahite kings: Josiah (639-609 BCE), his son Jehoiakim (609-598 BCE), and his other son

Zedekiah (598-587 BCE). His call to the work of a prophet came in the year 627 BCE, in the middle of the sweeping religious reforms being enacted by Josiah. The pressing danger Judah faced during this period was a growing threat from the Neo-Babylonian Empire, the power du jour that had recently displaced the Assyrians for dominance of the region. New empire, same story, unfortunately for the people of Israel and Judah. As the place where the Asian and African continents converged and bordered by the Mediterranean Sea (which leads to Europe), Israel was a sought-after piece of real estate by all the empires and want-to-be empires of the ancient world.

Israel was a sought-after piece of real estate by all the empires and want-to-be empires of the ancient world.

It's important to acknowledge that events rarely, if ever, happen in a vacuum. Today's headlines are usually rooted in happenings weeks, months, or even years before the contemporary moment. That is also true of the context of Jeremiah 29:11. To get the full picture of what it is that Jeremiah is responding to, we have to go back more than one hundred years to the time of the prophet Isaiah. In 701 BCE the kingdom of Judah faced the threat of one of the ancient world's most brutal empires, the Assyrians. Two decades before that, in 721 BCE, the Assyrians defeated Israel, Judah's sibling kingdom to the north. Many of the inhabitants of Israel were exiled to other lands in the Assyrian empire, and according to their policy, other peoples were brought in to repopulate the land that had been Israel.

You can imagine the terror that befell the nation of Judah, to the south, twenty years later when the Assyrians turned their focus onto their kingdom. Faced with the impending doom of Assyrian brutality, King Hezekiah prayed to God for help fending off their would-be conquerors. Because of that prayer, Isaiah the prophet assured the king, Assyria would not destroy Jerusalem. Instead, Assyria's proud rulers would meet the judgment of Judah's God. While historical sources disagree about the reasons for it, the Assyrians eventually fled having not conquered Jerusalem. Their king, Sennacherib, was eventually killed by his own sons, which for the people of Judah no doubt felt like a vindication of Isaiah's message.

This trip down memory lane is important for our understanding of Jeremiah's context. Roughly one hundred years later, there was a new empire calling the shots, the Babylonians. Judah, once again, was under threat of annihilation. However, this time, there was less concern about the possibility that the Babylonians would succeed. After all, Assyria had failed. How could anyone overthrow Jerusalem? The Temple of God was located there, and surely God would not allow the Temple to be destroyed. Not so fast, said Jeremiah. He warned that the Temple would not protect Judah from the Babylonians, because God was actually using Nebuchadnezzar of Babylon to hold Judah accountable.

Jeremiah's critique was that worshipping in the Temple was not a substitute for the implementation of justice. It is the lack of justice, and the practice of idolatry, that Jeremiah sees as the cause of all the problems facing the people. He reminded his Judahite listeners that Shiloh, the place of worship in Israel (the Northern Kingdom) was wiped out, so what would prevent God from allowing the Jerusalem Temple from experiencing the same fate?

The epitome of the squeaky wheel, Jeremiah persisted with his challenge to King Jehoiakim. The solution would not be rebellion against Babylon, but acceptance of Babylonian control, that would ultimately save the people. To refuse Babylon was to choose destruction, Jeremiah said. The king failed to heed the prophet's words, instead listening to other prophets (deemed false prophets by Jeremiah) who encouraged outright rebellion against Nebuchadnezzar. So, after three years under Babylonian subordination, King Jehoiakim of Judah rebelled. His hope was that Egypt would come to their aid against Babylon, but that would not happen. Egypt itself had fallen to Babylonian control.

After Jehoiakim's death, his son Jehoiachin would spend a brief three months on the throne. His reign was ended by Nebuchadnezzar laying siege to Jerusalem. To stave off total destruction, Jehoiachin surrendered. Not only did the Babylonians take the king captive, but they also pillaged the Temple's treasures and sacred vessels, and carried into exile the upper classes of Judahite society—officials, nobility, craftsman, and so forth. This was the first deportation of Judah to Babylon, occurring in the year 597 BCE. Ten years later, the Babylonians would come again to lay siege to Jerusalem. Next time the entire city would be destroyed, the Temple razed, and the people carried into exile in Babylon, leaving only the poorest to remain in the land.

JEREMIAH 29

This first deportation to Babylon is the key to understanding the context of Jeremiah 29, because it is a letter written from the prophet to those in that early exilic community in Babylon. We might think about the role of the prophet as twofold. First, a prophet has the task of warning and disturbing. That had been Jeremiah's work from his call to the vocation of prophet in 627 BCE to the time of the first deportation of exiles from Judah in 597 BCE. He was a burr in the saddle of those who refused to come to terms with the situation that Judah was facing. This wouldn't play out the way the Assyrian conflict did. Jeremiah's message in this case was one of impending doom. If the people did not abandon idols and pursue justice, then God would use Babylon as an instrument to correct course. Resistance was useless, because to fight Babylon was tantamount to fighting God. This message did not win many friends for Jeremiah. If his job was to convince those in power to accept Babylonian control, it could be said that he failed miserably.

However, that is only part of the prophetic task. First, there is the work of disturbance and warning. After disaster, the prophet does not come gloating, saying "I told you so." When their words are proven true, the prophet comes with a message of comfort and hope. That is what Jeremiah does in his letter to the initial exiles in Babylon.

The gist of the letter is twofold. First, he is writing to instill hope and to encourage the community. Second, he is writing to combat the notion being spread by other prophets that the exile in Babylon will be short-lived. This will not be the case, says Jeremiah. Knowing that this will be a long-term situation, Jeremiah offers the exilic community a kind of bad news/good news assessment of their new reality. He began with the bad news: Exile will last at least seventy years (he was slightly off, 597-538 BCE is only 59 years). He encouraged those who had been displaced to Babylon to settle down, to build a life there, and even to seek the "welfare of the city" (Jeremiah 29:4-7). They should ignore the voices that were saying it would be brief. Then came the good news: God had not abandoned or forgotten them in Babylon.

Once the time for Babylon's dominance had been completed, God would bring the people back to the land of their ancestors. This is the commitment that sparks the promise of verse 11.

THE PROMISE TO THE EXILIC COMMUNITY

While exile would not be brief, it would also not last forever, says the prophet. God had not forgotten the Judahite community in Babylon. Thus, the promise: "For surely I know the plans I have for you, says the LORD, plans for your welfare and not for harm, to give you a future with hope" (Jeremiah 29:11).

It's important for us to understand what is and isn't being said in this verse. Often, this is read as being an affirmation that God has a very specific plan for each individual human life. Like my experience as a teenager, the idea that God has a plan can be both comforting and unnerving. Comforting in that, God is aware and thinking about my life. Unnerving in that, if I miss a turn in the directions, my entire future could be derailed. Is that what the prophet is offering to the exilic community?

Let's begin with the idea of *plans*. In Hebrew the phrase *I know the plans I have for you* is actually best rendered as *I know the thoughts I think*. The difference in *plans* and *thoughts* is important. *Plans* seems, at least to me, to indicate something settled, set in stone. When we make plans, sure, anything could happen, but we at least know we are supposed to go to dinner or the movies or the sports game. The text of Jeremiah 29:11 isn't saying that. The concept could better be rendered as *intentions*. God has intentions for the exilic community. We might even say God has *hopes* for them. The idea that God plans everything, every detail of our lives, is problematic. It makes God the source of the good we experience and the bad. It also ignores and erases our own free will. If God has decided everything for us, then how can we ever be free to make a choice? Both our good deeds and our bad decisions are coerced.

The idea that God plans everything, every detail of our lives, is problematic.

In his letter to the exiles Jeremiah is offering them a hopeful view of God. This isn't a God who controls humanity. The reality of exile should dispel that rumor. What kind of God creates people and then decides for them that they will miss the mark? Jeremiah's point isn't that God willed the exile. God's intentions had always been that all the people flourish and thrive. Jeremiah's prophetic warning called them to make justice a priority:

> For if you truly amend your ways and your doings, if you truly act justly one with another, if you do not oppress the alien, the orphan, and the widow or shed innocent blood in this place, and if you do not go after other gods to your own hurt, then I will dwell with you in this place, in the land that I gave to your ancestors forever and ever.
>
> (Jeremiah 7:5-7)

It was their refusal to uphold justice that created the problem they were experiencing. The Exile was about removing the injustice from the land. Yet, God would also pursue them, even into Babylon, and would ensure they would once again be restored in their land.

God was still somehow with them, and somehow still had good intentions toward them, even when they were conquered and displaced. Both the longing for home and the sense of estrangement from their God is reflected in the words of the psalmist:

> By the rivers of Babylon—
>> there we sat down, and there we wept
>> when we remembered Zion.
> On the willows there
>> we hung up our harps.
> For there our captors
>> asked us for songs,
> and our tormentors asked for mirth, saying,
>> "Sing us one of the songs of Zion!"
>
> How could we sing the LORD's song
>> in a foreign land?
>
> (Psalm 137:1-4)

Their longing for home was met with God's intention to do just that, to carry them back home...eventually. In the meantime, God would not be distant or absent, according to Jeremiah. Far from it. The assumption, in the ancient world, was that gods were connected to the geography in which they were worshipped. God, then, was located in Judah, more specifically in the Jerusalem Temple. But that assumption, Jeremiah argues, is wrong. This God is among the exiles and can easily be found if they would seek with "all their heart" (Jeremiah 29:13 NIV).

Further, the thoughts God was thinking toward the exilic community were so that they may "prosper" (NIV), for their welfare (NRSVue), and for their peace (KJV). Sometimes words are so big, they contain so much meaning, that one word cannot contain their description. The Hebrew word being translated here, *shalom*, is one such word.

Shalom is often translated simply as *peace*, but that single word cannot hold all the meaning. When we think of peace, we usually think of the cessation of conflict. Peace is something that gets brokered between warring parties. *Shalom*, however, is the state of things when everything is in its right place and relationship. Other words that can be used, like *prosper*, *welfare*, *wholeness*, *harmony*, and *well-being* all bring specific elements of meaning to the forefront. My favorite word that attempts to draw them all together is *flourishing*. *Shalom* is what happens when all of creation—humans, animals, and planet—are all living in connection and cooperation. The Exile itself is an example of what can happen in communities when justice and the flourishing of all members of society are not prioritized.

As Jeremiah describes God's intention for *shalom* for Judah, we hear echoes of the second creation story in Genesis 2–3. Creation begins in harmony and partnership, between the Divine and the human, human and human, and humans and the planet. It begins in a state of vulnerability, the first humans naked and unashamed. Once the fruit of judgment had been consumed (which is what the "Knowledge of Good and Evil" is pointing toward), suddenly vulnerability is too big a risk. Humanity hides, from God and one another. The harmonious relationship shared by all creation is disrupted. The first humans are exiled from Eden. This is the story of Judah, isn't it? Living in the land of promise, stewards of the Temple of God, but not stewards of justice. Instead of cultivating *shalom*, they had fostered injustice. God's intention for the people was to return home, but not a return to business as usual. The dysfunction of the past must be replaced with *shalom*, so that all members of the community could flourish.

Not only did God have good intentions of *shalom* toward the exiles, but the verse ends with an interesting line. God would give them "a future with hope," says the NRSVue. This is a common way that translations have rendered this final part of verse 11. More literally the phrase can be rendered, to give them "an expected end." What might feel unending, won't be, Jeremiah comforts. The distance between the people and their land might feel insurmountable. The losses Exile brought might seem beyond repair. And this wouldn't be over quickly. Yet, there would be a coming day on which the people would, once again, go home. Jeremiah was quite good at the disturb-and-warn piece of the prophetic task, and in 29:11 we discover that he was also adept at the comfort-and-hope piece as well.

APPLYING JEREMIAH 29:11 TODAY

I know that, over the years, the way I and others have interpreted Jeremiah 29:11 has been done with the best of intentions. Perhaps even similar intentions to that of Jeremiah, to comfort and offer hope. I still think we can engage this text in this way, but I want to offer a few cautions, a few things to keep in the front of our minds as we seek to apply this text to our own contexts, today.

First, we have to remember that this text was originally a letter sent to a community of people who had been displaced from their land by the empire of their day. My context is extremely different from that of the original audience. The truth is, as a citizen of one of the wealthiest and most powerful empires the world has ever known, I have far more in common with the people in Babylon than I do the Judahite community that was taken there in exile. As a person of privilege, I must be careful when engaging passages like this to not appropriate the comfort and hope being offered to an oppressed group of people. Before I can extract some meaning for my own life and experience, it is imperative that I see the community that is being addressed, and as best I can, hear their experience and story.

This is why we've taken time in each of the chapters in this book to explore who the real human lives and communities were that first received these letters and stories. If we do not put in this work, we risk erasing the lives and experiences of real people and communities in an attempt to find some meaning for our own lives. However, if we do not rush past the details, if we hear the passages within the contextual light of the people who wrote and received them, it allows a deeper engagement—one that will challenge us to acknowledge the reality of our privilege and to hear God's concern for those who are on the underside of power.

Another concern when applying this text is that, in context, this passage speaks to a community, not to individuals. Jeremiah is not writing to comfort *an exile*, but the *exilic community* as a whole. I'm not trying to nitpick, here; I really think this awareness matters. Everything in our culture, it seems, is geared toward the individual. We are a society of individuals, and as such we place a high value on our individual experiences, needs, and wants. I don't think that's a bad thing. It is important, however, to acknowledge that the ancient world did not think this way, and as we enter ancient texts we have to keep that in mind. Jeremiah 29:11 is not just a promise to me or you that God has good thoughts toward us and wants to give us a future full of hope and flourishing. It's a promise to a community, collectively, about the kind of society they could be. That's because *shalom*—flourishing—is not an individual, solo experience. Flourishing is what happens when we, together, create a society that works toward justice for all. I can't do that alone, and neither can you. When we hear the promise of Jeremiah 29:11 through the filter of community it is full of hope and promise, but it also means that we have work to do. Flourishing doesn't just happen, it must be intentionally cultivated. For that to happen, we all must bring our individual creativity and experiences to join the community in solving the roadblocks to flourishing for everyone in the community. Yes, that feels like a daunting, almost impossible task. Which is why community is essential. What we cannot do on our own becomes possible when we work together.

Flourishing doesn't just happen,
it must be intentionally cultivated

A final important issue to keep in mind when we attempt to apply this text today is the lived experience of others. As a pastor for almost twenty-five years, I have had the honor of being with people on their best and worst days. I have celebrated marriages and births, graduations and dream jobs secured. Those are really good days and moments. Yet, I have also been on the other side of that coin, walking with people through their worst days. Being close to people who have experienced unfathomable loss and suffering has caused me to pay more attention to the way I speak about things like "God's plan," or how God intervened in a specific scenario.

Think about how it might feel, from the perspective of loss, to hear someone say, "God had it planned out for my good," when something bad was avoided. How might someone who just lost a loved one to cancer experience the idea of "God's plan for our good"? Would someone who lost a family member to a car accident feel excluded or hurt by someone saying that they came through unscathed because God was watching out for them?

I am not suggesting that it's inappropriate to be thankful for the good things that happen to us, or to even express that gratitude toward God. Of course, gratitude is a good thing. To be part of a community, like a church, means that we hold the expanse of human emotion. As Paul told the Corinthians, as the body of Christ, "if one member suffers, all suffer together with it; if one member is honored, all rejoice together with it" (1 Corinthians 12:26).

What I am suggesting is developing a sensitivity to the complexity of human life and experience. No matter how much we'd like to believe that everything is really simple—good things happen to good people, bad things to bad people—our lived experience of life tells us the opposite. Many wonderful people suffer. Lots of harmful people thrive. The rain does fall on the just and the unjust, and that is one of the most confusing and difficult realities we face. That struggle is found within the canon we call Scripture. There's the optimism of Proverbs, the pessimism of Ecclesiastes, and the confusion and awe of Job. Like Job's friends, we often want to make pronouncements and find answers, but the truth is sometimes it's just sitting in the mystery and pain of it all, knowing that it all matters and it's all holy.

Our responsibility toward one another is to extend compassion and kindness, and to act in ways that are loving and thoughtful. That's why I raise this awareness as an important consideration when we are attempting to apply this passage, today. Because love calls us to see and care for the pain of those around us and to minimize the ways we contribute to that pain.

DOES GOD HAVE A PLAN?

When I became a legal licensed driver, the world was a wildly different place. In the mid 90s cell phones were few and far between. Today, regardless of where I am going, or how well I know the way, I always end up putting the address in my one of my map apps. It keeps me aware of traffic, tells me when to slow down to avoid a speeding ticket (not that I'd ever speed), and constantly monitors traffic for the best, quickest route to my destination. Back then, when I just started driving, if I was unsure where I was going, I would just go online and print the step-by-step directions from MapQuest. I'd follow them closely, turn by turn, ensuring that I made it to my desired location.

The claim of Jeremiah 29:11 is not that God has a specific, individual plan for every single person, and that we must figure out what it is and try to live it out. There are no pre-scripted, step-by-step directions that we must follow. I also do not believe that God plans ease and luxury for some, while doling out suffering and misery for others. If that is true, what does it mean for God to have a plan, then?

I have really grown to love the idea of God having *intentions* toward us, even for us. Maybe we could even use the word *hope*. God has hopes for us, for how we will show up in the world toward God and one another, even toward the planet. God has intentions for us, that we would be shaped and formed in and by love, that we would be compassionate and just in the way we organize our common life together.

God, however, doesn't control the outcome. If God did then we wouldn't be free to choose. Our participation wouldn't matter. It's all a ruse. That's just not the case. The Exile experience itself proves that God won't force God's intention on people. We have always had the freedom and capacity to resist and reject God's intention toward us or for us. Which means, though God longs for justice, we can choose to create systems of inequity. While God is love, we can choose hate and bigotry as our way. Though God wills the flourishing of all humans, we can resist and work against it becoming a reality. That's not because God is weak, it's because God is love. Love demands the freedom to choose differently. Coercion can create fear that leads to obedience, but it doesn't inspire love that leads to transformation.

I have experienced this reality significantly as a parent. My wife and I have five kids, and each one is different, unique. Which means she and I have our own unique relationships with each one of them. What has been challenging for us is, as they've gotten older and started to become their own people, there is not a lot that is within our control. I don't mean we just let them run totally wild with no boundaries or expectations. What I mean is that they have to make choices about the kinds of people they are becoming. My oldest, especially, is at the age where I can no longer make those decisions for him. I can encourage, invite, challenge…all of that, but he has to decide who he wants to be, what kind of human he wants to be. My hope is that, throughout his life, we have pointed him in a good direction, and that he will make decisions consistent with the love in which he's being raised.

My experience as a parent has convinced me all the more that God's love requires the same from God. That for God to be love, and for us to be free to return or resist that love, God must have open hands toward us. That doesn't mean that God doesn't have dreams for us— the kinds of people we will be and the kind of world we will build. I believe deeply that God does. God dreams of a world where all of us flourish, where we all find the healing and wholeness that were meant to be ours. The hope of God is that we will be so transformed by love that we choose to partner with God to answer the prayer of Jesus, "on earth as it is in heaven."

The hope of God is that we will be so transformed by love that we choose to partner with God to answer the prayer of Jesus, "on earth as it is in heaven."

Jeremiah 29:11 reflects this deep hope of God. Through the prophet Jeremiah, God speaks comfort to a displaced people, longing for home. God has not forgotten you, the prophet says, nor has God abandoned you. God is with you, even in the disorientation of the Exile. Even now God has intentions toward you that are full of hope, flourishing, and the journey homeward. Then and now, the next move has always been ours. We get to decide if or how we partner with God to make God's intention a reality. The ball is in our court, so to speak.

Finally, Jeremiah 29:11 reflects the truth that God doesn't have a plan for my life, individually, as much as God has a plan for our lives, together. God has a dream for the kind of world we could create. You and I have invitations to, individually, show up and bring our creativity, skill, and uniqueness together to make that world possible. May we join our action with God's intention. May we participate to make God's dream a reality on earth, as it is in heaven.

"I Can Do All Things Through Him Who Strengthens Me"

Philippians 4:13

CHAPTER 5

"I Can Do All Things Through Him Who Strengthens Me"
(Philippians 4:13)

As I mentioned in the Introduction, one of the central reasons why many people read the Bible is to find encouragement, hope, and inspiration. In the words and stories of our ancient spiritual ancestors we search for wisdom that can empower and comfort us through the challenges life brings to us. I have found this to be true in my work as a pastor. In that role, I regularly talk to people who are trying to make sense of an experience they've had—often an experience of grief—or looking for encouragement as they are attempting something new and daunting. One of the questions I am often asked by these folks is about the Bible, specifically are there any verses I could recommend to offer them support and guidance. It's a natural desire for a person who finds meaning in the Bible to want to find ways to engage Scripture throughout the various ups and downs of life.

There are certain verses of Scripture that are so popular they get printed on home decor, clothing, coffee mugs, car vanity plates, and just about any other kind of knick-knack you can imagine. It's a big business. My task as a pastor is to help people do that, to find that encouragement and hope, in a way that doesn't distort or manipulate random passages by taking them out of context. It is a delicate process to balance both the need and impulse of the search for support and also to ensure that I am helping people engage Scripture in a way that I can stand behind.

One such verse that is cited again and again in the way I am describing is Philippians 4:13. While it belongs to Paul's letter to the Philippian church, it has become associated today with overcoming obstacles and challenges. It's equally claimed by students looking to pass a major exam, athletes who want to win the big game, and lots of others in between. And I can see why. Here are Paul's words in case they aren't familiar: "I can do all things through him who strengthens me" (Philippians 4:13).

Right? No wonder people who are facing difficult challenges find resonance in this verse. It makes a bold claim, that with God/Christ as the source of strength, all things can be done. *All* is a big word, isn't it? If you'll pardon a bad pun, it's *all* encompassing.

I recently had a catch-up Zoom call with a friend I hadn't seen in a while. When we logged on he was so excited to show me his brand new coffee mug. It wasn't anything special or eye-catching. Just a white ceramic mug, with a message spelled out in black letters: "I can do all things through a verse taken out of context." I immediately cackled. It's a brilliant idea. It's also true. We can and have done lots of things throughout Christian history—some really terrible things—because we have believed the Bible supported it. We have far too many times proof texted our way to atrocities and harm. In the process we have also become unfamiliar with the Bible, knowing only the "Greatest Hits," but not the situations and backgroundS that created them.

I don't think it's wrong or out of place to search for consolation or relief in the words of Scripture.

To show my cards at the beginning, I don't think it's wrong or out of place to search for consolation or relief in the words of Scripture. Of course not. At the same time, I do firmly believe it's important to know a bit about the context in and from which these passages come to us. It's a way of honoring the sources and communities that produced them, and a way of ensuring that we are not just creating a patchwork of verses that serve our ends. With that preamble, we now turn to explore the context of Philippians 4:13.

A LETTER OF LOVE

The city of Philippi played a significant role in the development of the Roman Empire. It was the site of the decisive battle in the Roman civil war after the assassination of Julius Caesar. In 42 BCE, the future emperor Augustus, then called Octavian, and his ally Marc Antony defeated the conspirators in Caesar's assassination. In the aftermath of the battle Rome settled military veterans there, and eventually Philippi was elevated to the status of a Roman colony—the highest status that a territory could be given. To be a Roman colony was to be a miniature Rome, to embody the culture and values of Rome. Paul tells the Philippians that they have a citizenship in heaven, meaning their values will place them into conflict with those of Rome (Philippians 3:20).

According to the Book of Acts, the Philippian church is the first Paul founded on the European continent. He went there after the Spirit, Acts 16 says, prevented him and his companions from taking their message to Asia. During that visit he also ran into trouble, and he ended up spending a brief time in jail for creating a public disturbance. Elsewhere, in Paul's own words, we learn about an experience where he was "shamefully mistreated" in Philippi (1 Thessalonians 2:2). The point is that Paul and the Philippians were not mere acquaintances. There was a deep connection between the two.

Philippians is different from Paul's other known letters. Most of the letters we have authentically from Paul were written to answer questions or specifically address problems within the fledgling Jesus communities that were beginning throughout the Roman Empire. Philippians isn't doing that. To be sure Paul does reference some trouble he's experienced and offers wisdom for the community about how to respond to those coming to them with different teaching than he gave them. He also calls out a situation between two women in the Philippian church, Euodia and Syntyche, leaders in the community, that concerned him. These women had worked—struggled he says—alongside him in his efforts, and he pleads with them to be "of the same mind in the Lord" (Philippians 4:2).

Try to imagine the scene with me. A letter from Paul has just arrived, and there's a palpable buzz in the community as everyone anticipates what he will say. Then, toward the end of the letter, you hear your name, and the name of someone you've not been getting along with, called out in front of everyone. Talk about embarrassing! Added to that is the fact that for almost two thousand years their disagreement has been read about and talked about by billions of people. I'm sure they would have preferred a little more discretion from Paul.

That notwithstanding, Philippians isn't doing the same thing as, say, the Corinthian letters. Paul isn't writing because he needs to wade into the waters of church drama and conflict and attempt to sort it out. Overall, Philippians has a totally different vibe. This letter is drenched in affection, gratitude, and joy. It's also what Paul thought would be his swan song. Philippians is a farewell letter from the founder of the community to his beloved congregation, from a Roman prison.

A LETTER FROM PRISON

The location for this imprisonment is up for debate, because it's not clear in the letter from where Paul is writing. There are three potential locations for Paul's imprisonment. A majority of scholars think he was writing in the mid 50s from Ephesus. It's evident from his writings that Paul had spent time there and that it wasn't always sunshine and roses—he apparently fought "wild beasts" in Ephesus, according to 1 Corinthians 15 (verse 32 NIV). However, other scholars suggest a date in the late 50s in Caesarea, while others assert it was written from the Roman imprisonment in the early 60s, not long before his death. Regardless of where he wrote it, Philippians indicates that Paul believed that his time was growing short, and that his life would soon end because of his proclamation of the gospel. Undaunted by his present circumstances, and the potential for his life to end, Paul reminds the Philippians that from his perspective, "For to me, to live is Christ and to die is gain" (Philippians 1:21 NIV).

Paul's context in prison makes the tone and content of Philippians all the more surprising. Throughout this short letter, comprised of only 104 verses, Paul used the words for joy and rejoicing sixteen times. He keeps bringing the community back to the necessity of making space for joy, even when their present circumstances, like his, are difficult. While he might be in chains, the message of Jesus could not be stopped, and that, for Paul, was the source of much rejoicing.

From his writings we know that Paul was no stranger to prison or challenging circumstances. He had been beaten and abused, imprisoned and shipwrecked, and that is just the tip of the iceberg. In 2 Corinthians 11 he recounts the constant danger, hard work, and conflict he experienced as a result of his ministry. He told the Corinthians that he had experienced "many a sleepless night, [been] hungry and thirsty, often without food, cold and naked" (v. 27). In the Roman era, prisoners would have been dependent on family and friends to supply their needs for food, water, and clothing while in prison. In the absence of support from one's community, the experience would be very much what Paul described to the Corinthians. Enter the Philippian church and their concern for their founder and friend.

Based on Paul's side of the correspondence we can reconstruct a bit about his relationship to the church in Philippi, and why he felt compelled to write them such an affectionate letter. When word of his imprisonment reached the Philippians, they didn't sit idly by or just offer some thoughts and prayers. They sprang into action, sending Epaphroditus to visit Paul and to deliver gifts to supply his needs. Thanking the Philippians for this generous act, and trying to calm their concern for his situation, is the central purpose of Paul's letter.

Some of the churches Paul had relationships with were known to be wealthy. The Corinthians, for example, were considered to be well off. This fact explains Paul's frustration with them in his second letter to the community. The churches Paul had responsibility for had been asked to take up a collection to send to the Jerusalem church, because they were experiencing difficult times and needed the support. However, the Corinthians, who had an abundance, were not quick to follow through with that work. When Paul addressed the issue, he used the Macedonian churches—the region in which Philippi was located, as an example of how to do the offering well.

> We want you to know, brothers and sisters, about the grace of God that has been granted to the churches of Macedonia, for during a severe ordeal of affliction their abundant joy and their extreme poverty have overflowed in a wealth of generosity on their part.
>
> 2 Corinthians 8:1-2

Notice the way Paul describes the generosity of churches like Philippi, with almost shockingly contradictory language. He brings together what seem to be opposites: severe affliction and abundant joy, extreme poverty and a wealth of generosity. Paul's point was clear, the Corinthians could be—should be—leading the way in terms of generosity, but it is actually their siblings who have the least that are contributing all that they could to encourage and support the Jerusalem church. Paul also reminds the Corinthians that while he was with them, they didn't support his work financially at all. It was actually the churches in Macedonia, including the Philippians, who provided for his needs. Taken together, an obvious pattern of Philippian generosity emerges. They had a deep love for Paul, and that was intensified all the more by their growing concern for his health and well-being while locked away because of his proclamation of the gospel.

I can imagine the relief Paul must have experienced when a friend from Philippi arrived with food, ointments, fresh clothing, and perhaps equally important, the love and encouragement of the community he founded. Sometime after his arrival Epaphroditus fell gravely ill, to the point of death. It seems that word of his sickness traveled quickly, and his community grew concerned for his well-being. Fortunately, by the time Paul wrote his letter to the community Epaphroditus had made a full recovery, and he would be the carrier of Paul's gratitude to the community. This desire to express his thanks, update them on his circumstances, and assuage their fears about his situation are the backdrop to Philippians chapter 4, to which we now turn.

PUTTING PHILIPPIANS 4:13 IN CONTEXT

Paul begins the chapter with an acknowledgment of and gratitude for the gift he had received. He wants them to know, however, that his experiences have taught him an interior expansiveness that allow him to be flexible and grounded regardless of the circumstances he finds himself moment by moment. He explains,

> *Not that I am referring to being in need, for I have learned to be content with whatever I have. I know what it is to have little, and I know what it is to have plenty. In any and all circumstances I have learned the secret of being well-fed and of going hungry, of having plenty and of being in need. I can do all things through him who strengthens me.*
>
> (Philippians 4:11-13)

Reading this passage with the standard interpretation in mind reminds me of the 1998 movie *The Waterboy*. The plot centers on a Louisiana college football team that is just plain awful, and the team waterboy who eventually becomes the star player that leads them to victory. In the movie there is a background character played by Rob Schneider who continually shows up and declares, "You can do it!" Is that what Paul is doing in this passage, like a coach giving a pep talk to their overmatched team, trying to make them believe they can do anything, even win the game? Is Paul declaring that there's no obstacle too great to overcome, no mountain too high to climb, no river too deep to cross for those who believe in Jesus? Is Paul creating a prototype of an inspirational poster, like the one with a kitten barely clinging to a rope with the text, *HANG IN THERE!*, written across the bottom? What is this secret that Paul claims to have discovered that enables him to have the confidence that he can do anything through the empowerment of Jesus?

What is this secret that Paul claims to have discovered that enables him to have the confidence that he can do anything through the empowerment of Jesus?

First, Paul uses an interesting word here that gets translated as "secret." It's the word *mueomai*, and it was a technical term used for initiation into a mystery religion in the ancient world. By the time we get to Paul the word was used, at times, more generally to describe a kind of insight or knowing that could come only through revelation by God. In other words, this *secret* Paul had been let in on wasn't something he just picked up through his travels. There was no class he attended or book he read that unlocked the wisdom he now possessed. This insight came through his connection to God, and it seems to have provided Paul a great deal of comfort. This secret knowledge was surely the source of Paul's capacity for joy even within his imprisonment, and it led him to a calm confidence, a kind of steadiness, that God's presence and peace would sustain and empower him to remain hopeful and peaceful in his varying circumstances.

What was this secret? Paul does a terrible job of keeping it quiet. He desperately wants to share this discovery with his friends in Philippi as they seek to process not only his difficult circumstances, but also their own. The content of the secret Paul has learned varies based on the translation from which we read. Notice the slight but significant differences we find across several widely used versions:

I can do all things through him who strengthens me. (NRSVue)

I can do all this through him who gives me strength. (NIV)

For I can do everything through Christ, who gives me strength. (NLT)

I have the strength for everything through him who empowers me. (NAB)

I can endure all these things through the power of the one who gives me strength. (CEB)

Did you notice the differences in these renderings of this verse? They are subtle, a word difference here or there, mainly in regard to what exactly it is that Paul can do. Is it all things? All this? Everything? The main glaring difference is between the last two options, the New American Bible and Common English Bible, and the rest. In those translations there is a lack of familiarity. They contain an echo of the standard translation, but if someone read only one of those versions and asked us for the chapter and verse, it might take us some time to get there.

While it probably sounds foreign it might surprise you to know that, of all the versions we looked at above, the NAB and CEB come the closest to the Greek text. I know, I know. It really shocked me too. The Greek text reads like this (I am sharing it in its unpolished form): "All things I am strong for in the one strengthening me."

It has a different ring to it, doesn't it? This isn't a declaration from Paul that he has learned how to overcome all obstacles and escape all suffering through strong, deep faith in Jesus. The claim isn't that, if you just believe enough, Jesus will magically transform your situation into something far more pleasing or manageable. Instead, Paul says that the secret he has been privy to is that in every situation in which he finds himself, both abundance and scarcity or suffering and joy, he is strengthened and empowered to be content in whatever the circumstance.

It's important to note here that this doesn't mean that Paul was *hoping* for misery or suffering. I imagine if we could sit Paul down for a conversation he, like us, would express a preference for abundance and joy over scarcity and suffering. Yet, Paul's words reflect the reality of our human existence. Our lives are complicated and complex. Our experiences, even the best or worst of them, are not linear or simple. So often joy and grief are not mutually exclusive experiences, but simultaneous ones.

This reality is reflected and experienced in all sorts of ways. As a parent I regularly experience the emotional tension of watching my kids grow up. In one sense, seeing them become more independent, self-sufficient, and mature is a joy. It's how it works, isn't it? They are supposed to be growing and maturing. There's also a grief that is bound up in that experience. Every milestone is a reminder that, one day, we will be empty-nesters, and our kids will have lives that we are part of but aren't centered on our family life anymore. It hits me in my feels just typing these words. There's both joy and grief at the same time.

I often think about the final speech Martin Luther King Jr. gave on the eve of his assassination in Memphis in 1968. Rallying on behalf of striking sanitation workers, King used the speech to call for, in the words of the prophet Amos, justice that rolls down like waters (see Amos 5:24). At the end of the speech King evoked the image of the Israelites crossing into the Promised Land after their wilderness wandering. In that story Moses, the liberator, is allowed to go up on a mountaintop to see, but not enter, the land. He concluded the speech with the joy that, eventually, his people would enter the land of promise, even though he knew that it was a very real possibility that he would not live to see that happen. In King's final address, joy and grief are sitting side by side.

It's a similar experience for Paul that is being expressed in Philippians 4:13. As he sits in a jail cell, unsure of his fate, he is awash with emotion. Surely he felt grief, and some fear. He was a human being, after all. That he was simultaneously being buoyed by joy and hope is also evident. That experience, the joy and hope in the midst of grief and fear, Paul called "the peace of God, which surpasses under-standing" (Philippians 4:7). His sense of Jesus's and the Philippians' companionship in his suffering enabled him to face the uncertainty of his predicament with resolve and courage.

Christ didn't always empower and strengthen Paul so that he could escape all weakness. Weakness, Paul knew, was part of the human experience. In his world, like ours, weakness was seen as something to be masked—you would never announce or emphasize a weakness. The transformation of how he viewed weakness was part of his experience of Jesus. Paul was aware that one pushback on the Jesus story meant that he failed. Jesus did not defeat Rome, he was defeated. That wasn't the end of the story, Paul knew, but he also sought to reframe what that defeat and the perceived weakness it illuminated meant.

While the message of the cross was foolish to some, for Paul it was transformative.

While the message of the cross was foolish to some, for Paul it was transformative. Some crosses cannot be avoided, he knew. Yet, his experience of Jesus led him to experience a source of strength that enabled him to face and endure the worst of his sufferings. In context, then, Paul is not celebrating that he will always overcome the challenges that he might face. Far from it. He is sharing the secret of his ability to keep going, even when the outcome is not something for which he wished or hoped. In both the joy and pain, victory and defeat, Paul was being empowered to keep going by the Jesus who had become Paul's source of strength.

THE GOOD NEWS OF PHILIPPIANS 4:13

At this point you might wonder why I'd want to make a big deal about putting Philippians 4:13 in context. Why is it a problem if we just allow this verse to be a source of "You can do it!" inspiration in the face of adversity? Primarily, my concern is that, when divorced from its context, this verse can become a source of shame, blame, and guilt that are unnecessary and not ours to carry.

My youngest daughter has spina bifida, which for her means limited mobility among some other impacts. A few years ago, a local nonprofit reached out to us and invited us to apply for her to receive a dream vacation, and if selected, they would send our entire family of seven on an all-expenses-paid trip to wherever she dreamed to go. She didn't have to think very long about her pick. Right away, she said, "Disney!" We turned in her paperwork and were totally shocked to learn that her dream had been granted, and we, like many a Super Bowl champion team before us, were going to Disney World. Perhaps the best thing about the trip was the Genie Pass. It looked, as you might imagine, like the Genie from *Aladdin*, and it meant that the Scott crew didn't have to wait in a single line. We'd walk up to a line that wrapped around and around, some with advertised wait times of more than two hours, and we'd get into the express lane, bypass all the other people, and get to ride first. We'd walk by and people would look at us the way the Grinch looked at all the Whos in Whoville. They weren't thrilled about it, but we had the Genie Pass and it would've been silly not to use it.

For us, It. Was. Magical.

It also gave our kids some unrealistic expectations about the whole Disney experience. The lines really are super long. Next time I know our trip will be full of "How much longer?" and "Can we go somewhere else?" Our dream experience did not encapsulate so much of the reality of a trip to Disney. I tell you this story because I think that's how some of us have been told life works when you are faithful or believe the right things about God/Jesus/the Bible, etc. If we have enough faith, all the red lights turn green, the cop doesn't stop us for speeding, we get a clean bill of health, make a ton of money, ace the exam . . . you get the idea. Jesus becomes kind of a magical talisman that lets us skip all the lines and removes all the obstacles that are in our way. But that's not how any of this works.

When our assumption about this verse is that it means we "can do everything through Christ," then what happens when we do everything within our power and still experience failure? What do we do if we don't overcome all the challenges or obstacles we face? Who is to blame? Could it be anyone but us? Too often when a person's experience and the standard interpretation of Scripture don't add up we immediately blame the person instead of interrogating our understanding of Scripture. It is far easier to believe that someone else is wrong or does not have enough faith than it is to face the truth that it's possible that our interpretation doesn't match how reality works. There are scores of people who have suffered great pain or loss only to have that compounded by being blamed for the outcome, which may have never been in their hands to begin with.

Failure, weakness, and defeat are not always indicative that we have done something wrong. They don't mean we didn't have enough faith, or that we didn't try hard enough. The story of Jesus is one that includes defeat and weakness. You can have deep faith and couple that with hard work and dedication, and you will still, at some point, taste the bitterness of failure. The promise of Philippians 4:13 has never been that if you believe the "right things" you'll never lose or grieve or faceplant. It's never been a guarantee that, if you just get all your doctrinal ducks lined up in a row you'll never taste failure. The promise has always been strength and empowerment, even in moments of loss, grief, and failure.

In my experience, shame has rarely empowered or encouraged someone to keep going in the face of failure or difficulty. It's an interesting, albeit unhelpful, human impulse to look for something, or someone, to blame. I am more and more convinced that we heap shame upon others as a way of trying to help ourselves feel better about our own shortcomings and failures. If we just focus on *them*, then we don't have to deal with *us*. When the Bible is added into the mix, too often words that should be liberating and healing become a source of wounding and harm. Part of engaging the Bible responsibly is to think about the human impact of our readings, and to hold our interpretations with humility and curiosity.

Philippians 4:13 is a meaningful, encouraging verse of Scripture, even today. It is not a promise of success or a guarantee that we will overcome all the challenges that come before it. That just isn't how life works. All guarantees come with fine print. However, it is the good news that the same Jesus who empowered Paul and the Philippians in their struggles back then is also the same Jesus from whom we receive strength and encouragement today. In the ups and downs, the successes and failures, the joy and grief, we are not alone. We are seen, loved, and empowered to keep going.

THE SOURCE OF STRENGTH

How is that Paul knew Jesus as a source of empowerment and strength? I imagine in part it was an internal, even emotional sense for him. He felt Jesus with him and drew strength from that reality. I believe that to be true. However, I think another integral piece of that experience was Paul's communities, friends, and partners in his work. It should not be lost on us that it is in a letter to a community of people who had thoughtfully and generously showed up for him that Paul shares the secret to finding peace in the abundance and lack of life. The support of the Philippians must have been such an encouragement to Paul in his uncertain circumstances. In my own experience, it has been through people that time and time again God has provided the support, encouragement, and strength that Paul knows in Philippians 4:13.

Every time I have met God in any tangible way, God was always wearing human skin.

In my own life, and in the communities I have pastored, the way I have experienced anything close to what Paul is talking about is through the love, compassion, empathy, and kindness of other human beings. Humans who show up with a casserole. Humans who pay an electric bill or buy groceries. Humans who sit by the hospital bed or at the funeral home to be a compassionate presence. Humans who take seriously their role as God's Image Bearers in the world, being the presence of God to others in need. Every time I have met God in any tangible way, God was always wearing human skin.

Paul knew this firsthand through the kindness of his Philippian siblings. Their concern for him in the past, as they supported his ministry, and now, as they provide for his needs in prison, were a tangible expression of encouragement and strength. That's why Paul could close his "thank-you" letter to them by saying, "And my God will fully satisfy every need of yours according to his riches in glory in Christ Jesus"(Philippians 4:19), because in Paul's experience this community would care for one another, and be the presence of Jesus to one another, as they had been to him.

This is where faith gets really, really practical. Ultimately, the point is not sitting around arguing about doctrinal matters and trying to decide who is most "right." Faith, in the way of Jesus and Paul, is about practically and compassionately embodying the love and care of God for our neighbors, wherever and whoever they may be. Through this lens, faith is not something that we possess by believing in certain theologies or interpretations. It is the living out of God's love for everyone and everything around us. This is a significant responsibility, as Paul knew. Yet, he remained confident that the Philippians were up to the challenge. I believe we are too.

CHAPTER 6

Sodom
and
Gomorrah

Genesis 19

CHAPTER 6

Sodom and Gomorrah

(Genesis 19)

We have arrived at the final chapter. We have one last text to place in context, and of the passages we have focused on in this book, this is the most important. My original outline was in chronological order, meaning we would have started with this chapter. However, I felt it best to save this story for last for two reasons. First, this story is the heaviest and most difficult of the six texts we have examined. Starting here, I was concerned, might have been too much too soon.

Second, this story—the destruction of the cities of Sodom and Gomorrah—is the most extreme example of how failure to understand the context of the Bible can lead to real harm being done to real people. This story has been used, perhaps more than any other, to exclude, demonize, and shame members of the LGBTQ+ community, and this is not a problem of the past. It still happens to this very day. Whether it's from hateful street preachers holding signs, internet commenters, and so many more in between, the specter of Sodom has loomed large and been used as a proof text to condemn. Sadly, this is a text with a body count. We cannot even begin to calculate the damage that has been done to real, beloved human beings because of what I believe to be a non-contextual reading of the story of Sodom in Genesis 19.

This story has been used, perhaps more than any other, to exclude, demonize, and shame members of the LGBTQ+ community.

The standard (but not the most ancient) interpretation of the story of Sodom and Gomorrah's destruction is that God annihilated the inhabitants of these cities because of their sexual orientation. Specifically, in this understanding, God destroyed Sodom and Gomorrah because the people who lived there engaged in same-sex relationships. Is this the best interpretation of the passage? Does it take into account the culture and context of the ancient world that serve as the background for the events of Genesis 19? How does the rest of the Bible understand the meaning of the Sodom story? These are the questions to which we now turn.

Two quick disclaimers before we move forward. First, I highly encourage you to take a moment and read the story of Sodom in Genesis 19:1-29. Knowing the shape and narrative of the story will be helpful to keep in mind as we continue. Second, this story is rated M for mature. As a result, there will be themes that emerge in this chapter that involve sexual assault, rape, and violence. To really understand the story of Sodom in its ancient context it is necessary to dive deeply into what is happening in the narrative, and how ancient readers might have heard it. Reader discretion is advised.

A CITY WITH A BAD REPUTATION

That the writers of the Bible had a less than favorable opinion of Sodom is not really up for debate. The first mention of Sodom occurs in Genesis 13, when Abram (later, Abraham) and his nephew Lot decided to part company because their possessions were becoming too great and creating conflict. Abram left the decision to Lot; wherever he decided to go, Abram would go in the opposite direction. Lot made the choice to go toward the east. This is a decision that should have all the alarms going off for us, because this references a recurring motif in Scripture—the idea that moving eastward is moving toward exile.

This pattern first occurs in Genesis 3, when the first humans are exiled from the Garden of Eden. They are sent to the east. A chapter later, after Cain commits the first named sin in the Bible by killing his brother Abel, he is sent to the land of Nod, again, east of Eden. This movement culminates in Genesis 11, with the Tower of Babel. The eastward migration landed humans at a place called Shinar, where they constructed a tower that could reach into the heavens. Not so subtly we are being told to pay attention to the movement east, because it always leads to exile and trouble.

In Lot's case this eastward movement took him to Sodom. The writer of Genesis 13:13 here foreshadows what will come six chapters later with the assessment that "the people of Sodom were wicked, great sinners against the LORD." The assessment of Genesis is that this movement east had placed Lot in the wrong place at the wrong time. This is further cemented in the conversation between God and Abram that occurs in Genesis 18. When God lets Abram in on what is coming for Sodom the reason for the city's impending doom is the impact they are having on others. God says to Abram, "How great is the outcry against Sodom and Gomorrah and how very grave their sin!" (Genesis 18:20). Whatever is happening in Sodom, it hasn't stayed in Sodom. The sin of the city had spilled over and was causing deep and serious problems.

UNDERSTANDING THE ANCIENT WORLD

Before we dig into the Sodom story in Genesis 19, it would be helpful to explore a similar story that can shed more light onto how the ancient world thought. One of the most important values commonly held was the concept of *xenia* (pronounced "zenia") or "guest-friendship." Connected to the Greek word for "stranger" (*xenos*), it focused on the responsibility incumbent on all people to practice hospitality toward others, especially strangers. For example, in a world without hotels and restaurants, travelers were totally dependent on the kindness and hospitality of others. It was the expectation that people would provide those passing through their town or village with a safe place to stay, food and drink, and a bath if asked. In return, guests were expected to not bring harm or threat to their host, to not be a burden, to regale them with stories of their travels, and to return the favor if given the chance. This understanding of guest-friendship was not just a good idea, or something that was strongly suggested. I know this sounds strange to many of us, but in the ancient world this was a moral imperative with serious consequences, as we will see.

This example, similar to the Sodom story, comes from a work known as *Metamorphoses* by the Roman poet Ovid. He tells a story about a couple, Baucis and Philemon, who understand the critical importance of *xenia*. Unbeknownst to the couple at first, but known to us, they play hosts to two of their gods, Zeus and Hermes. The gods arrived in their village disguised as peasant travelers, and begin asking the people of the town, known for being wealthy, for a place to stay. Remember, according to the conventions surrounding *xenia*, this is not an unreasonable request. It is the shared societal norm. However, no one would open their home to the incognito gods.

Finally, Zeus and Hermes knock on the door of a poor couple, Baucis and Philemon, who gladly open their home to the gods, even though they are unaware of the significance of the guests they were hosting. The poor couple supply their guests with a generous meal of food and wine, and Baucis notices that, although she has poured and poured wine into their cups, her pitcher remained full. This is all it took for the ruse to be up. They immediately realize they are hosting and eating with gods.

The gods respond to their hospitality by telling them that disaster is coming. Due to the lack of hospitality they experienced, the entire village would be destroyed. The generous couple should leave immediately to avoid the impending calamity. They should flee to the mountain, and not look back until they reached their destination. Baucis and Philemon obeyed the divine warning, and upon reaching the top of the mountain looked back over their village. It was completely destroyed by flood. The simple home they shared had been transformed by the gods into an elaborate temple. As a further reward for their practice of *xenia*, the couple were made to be the stewards of the temple. Eventually they died together, and afterward they became a pair of intertwined trees, locked in eternal embrace.

One of the reasons *xenia* was so crucial to the ancients is highlighted in this story. You never knew who the person in need at your door really was. It could be a human, but it could also be a god in disguise. This trope of entertaining gods unawares is a common theme in the ancient world, and it's an idea that even finds its way into the Bible. The author of the Book of Hebrews reminds readers, "Do not neglect to show hospitality to strangers, for by doing that some have entertained angels without knowing it" (Hebrews 13:2). As Baucis and Philemon (and their fellow villagers) discovered, responding to the gods with hospitality brought reward. To fail in hospitality brought destruction.

Does this story sound familiar? The characters, of course, are different, as are some of the story specific details. Yet, this story contains many similarities with the story of Sodom. It centers on divine visitors looking for shelter. There is a hostile populace who refuse to practice hospitality, and one specific family who embody the values of *xenia*. As a result of the city's action (or better, inaction) destruction is decreed. The hospitable family is given safe passage to escape what is coming upon their village. As they flee, they are told to not look back as the city is destroyed. There's even someone turned into a different form; in the case of Sodom, it's Lot's wife.

I submit that these stories both reflect how ancient peoples thought about the importance of practicing hospitality. That is clearly true of the story of Baucis and Philemon, but it is also true of the biblical story of Sodom as well. The emphasis on providing safety, shelter, and food, with such extreme consequences, might seem to us a little overblown, but in the ancient world that gave us the stories of the Bible, like the story of Sodom, it was an absolutely central and essential practice.

THE REAL SIN OF SODOM

To state it plainly up front, the sin of Sodom was not that the people of Sodom were LGBTQ+ or that they engaged in same-sex sexual relationships. The sin of Sodom was failing to practice hospitality— they did not welcome or care for the strangers who visited them. One of the first pushbacks against this understanding that I often receive focuses on the key detail difference between Baucis and Philemon and the story of Sodom: In Sodom the people attempted to have sex with the angelic visitors. How can this story be about hospitality when it seems so clear, the argument goes, that God is punishing the city because of their sexual appetite?

---

*The sin of Sodom was failing
to practice hospitality*

To answer that question, let's briefly walk through the story. In Genesis 18, three visitors come to see Abraham (his name was changed in chapter 17), and he and his wife quickly welcome them and prepare a meal for them. To put it another way, Abraham and Sarah practice the cultural norm of hospitality toward their guests. These weren't ordinary visitors, however. The narrative begins by telling us that "The LORD appeared to Abraham," meaning that these visitors are to be understood as representing God in the story.

God decides to tell Abraham that Sodom's chickens are coming home to roost. The outcry against the city because of the sin they perpetuate is so great that God is forced to take matters into God's own hands; the city must be destroyed. In response, Abraham does something remarkable. "Shall not the Judge of all the earth do what is just?" (Genesis 18:25) he asks God. How could God wipe out the righteous with the unrighteous? How could that be even remotely just? The bargaining began. Abraham, like an expert auctioneer, began throwing out numbers. How few righteous people had to be found in Sodom before God would spare them? Abraham began with fifty, but he was also persistent. God eventually agreed that for the sake of ten righteous people—a word that implies doing justice, not doctrinal purity—God would relent on the plans for Sodom's demolition.

When two of the men, who we are meant to understand as either angels of God or perhaps even God, arrive at the city, they are met at the gate by Lot. Remember, Lot is not from Sodom originally. He's a new transplant to the city, an immigrant. Upon seeing the visitors at the gate Lot sprang into hospitality mode. He offered to host them, to provide food, the safety of shelter, and a place to wash up. At first the visitors refuse, instead opting to sleep in the town square. This didn't set well with Lot. He seemed almost nervous about the idea. Lot insisted they stay with him, and his persistence paid off. They entered his home and his protection and began to feast.

Just as they were about to turn in for the evening, the people of Sodom, down to the last person we are told, surrounded Lot's house. They began to demand that Lot send out his guests so that they might "know" them—that's "know" in the biblical sense. Lot once again shifted into host mode and reminded the mob around his home that these people were his guests, and as such they had "come under the shelter of [his] roof" (Genesis 19:8). It's here that Lot does the unthinkable. He offers, instead, to give the demanding rabble his virgin daughters to do to them whatever they wished. The horror of this offer cannot be overstated. Lot, in an awful situation, makes it infinitely worse by offering his own daughters to the rapacious crowd. This suggestion feels to the people of Sodom like an insult. "This fellow came here as an alien," they say, "and he would play the judge!" (19:9).

Finally, as they pressed in against the door, attempting to break it down, Lot's guests pulled him inside and gave him an order to take everyone attached to him and to flee the city. The next day they made their escape to the hills outside the city. Infamously, his wife looked back and became a pillar of salt.

Now, let's return to the question of meaning. How could this story possibly be about hospitality when it seems to be about sex, particularly the desire of the men of Sodom to have sex with Lot's visitors? To begin with, the story is replete with the conventions of ancient guest-friendship hospitality. Lot encounters strangers (and he doesn't seem to know they are divine until it is revealed to him along with the news that the city is going to be destroyed) and welcomes them into his home for food, a bath, and safety. These are the hallmarks of ancient hospitality, as we've seen. He then places himself at odds with the entire city when he protects his guests from their ill intent. Finally, his family is given safety in return for their generosity to the divine visitors to whom they had opened their home. All those key details check all the boxes of ancient hospitality norms.

In addition, the people of Sodom did not come to Lot's house to have sex with his visitors. They came to rape them. This is not a story about consensual same-sex relationships, but about one group of people attempting to dominate and humiliate others in order to assert their power over them. This is not about *attraction*. It's not about a desire to be in a same-sex relationship. The reality is the ancient world had no category for sexual orientation in the way we do today. That doesn't mean that LGBTQ+ people didn't exist in the ancient world. They most certainly did. What it means is that they did not have developed categories for understanding and talking about things like sexual orientation or gender identity. This story is about hostility and hate toward the outsider.

Remember, as Lot fended off their demands the crowd reminds him that he too, is a foreigner to the city. I imagine this to be a not-so-veiled threat from this mob to Lot: Give us what we want, or we'll come after you, too. This is not a story about sexual orientation, or even the act of sex. It's a story about being hateful and hostile to strangers who are in need. It's a story of attempted rape and sexual assault in the service of domination. After all, are we to assume that Sodom was a city only comprised of men? Are we to believe that every man in Sodom was gay? Of course not. Yet, the whole of Sodom is overthrown as a response to their actions. That is a clue for us, pointing us in the direction of the real sin of Sodom.

The attempted sexual assault in Sodom is not an isolated event in human history. The rape of prisoners and enemies has been documented as an abhorrent practice, used to humiliate and torture. What we see in Sodom is not an issue of a few individuals engaging in hostility, but a societal problem. The outcry against Sodom had become ear-piercing, which means these visitors were not the first to come to the city in search of guest-friendship, only to find hate and violence. To miss this is to miss the central warning of the story.

What, then, can we say was the actual sin committed by the inhabitants of Sodom? If you recall, the word *xenia* comes from the Greek word *xenos*, which means "stranger." The problem is Sodom can be partly described as xenophobia, the fear of strangers. Instead of seeing people passing through town and in need of hospitality, the people of Sodom saw them as threats that needed to be preemptively dealt with. In short, the story of Sodom and Gomorrah isn't about who you love, it's about the refusal to love.

This becomes all the more glaring when we take just a moment to compare the hospitality of Abraham and Lot to the lack of it in Sodom. Both Abraham and Lot, without question, welcome and care for the strangers who visit them, keeping with the conventions of ancient hospitality practice. The people of Sodom do the opposite. They are not indifferent to strangers in need. Far from it. They prey upon the strangers in their midst. The hostility, inhospitality, and xenophobia of the people of Sodom created a culture in which outsiders were abused and traumatized. That is the sin of Sodom.

CALLING IN BACKUP

I can hear some of the skeptical responses to this interpretation. Aren't you just trying to justify same-sex relationships by reinterpreting the Bible to fit your agenda, some might ask? It is a fair question. The answer is a resounding "NO." When we do even a cursory survey of how the rest of the Bible speaks about the story of Sodom's destruction, the case that it is about the lack of hospitality and not human sexuality is only strengthened. We will briefly look at four examples, three from the Hebrew prophets and one from the Gospel of Matthew.

121

We begin in the work of the prophet Isaiah. In chapter 1, the prophet is calling out the people of Judah for forsaking the Lord through their refusal to enact justice. He calls their leaders "rulers of Sodom," and offers this prescription for solving their problem:

> *Wash yourselves; make yourselves clean;*
> > *remove your evil deeds*
> > *from before my eyes;*
> *cease to do evil;*
> > *learn to do good;*
> *seek justice;*
> > *rescue the oppressed;*
> *defend the orphan;*
> > *plead for the widow.*
> > > (Isaiah 1:16-17)

In these words, Isaiah diagnoses both the sin of Sodom and the sin of Judah as being a refusal to do what is just toward the oppressed, the orphan, and the widow. He is not alone in making this connection; the prophet Amos agrees. In chapter 4, Amos is talking to the wealthy and powerful of Israel "who oppress the poor, who crush the needy" (v. 1), and he name-drops Sodom (v. 11). Israel is on par with Sodom, he says, and many of them will meet the same fate that Sodom did, total destruction.

Next, we come to the prophet Ezekiel. Writing during the time of the Babylonian Exile, he compares Jerusalem, the religious, economic, and political center of the nation of Judah, to a "faithless bride." Time and again, God had provided for and doted on the nation, but time and again the people had been unfaithful to God in return. It is here that Ezekiel offers a harsh comparison. In chapter 16 he writes:

*As I live, says the Lord G*OD, *your sister Sodom and her daughters have not done as you and your daughters have done. This was the guilt of your sister Sodom: she and her daughters had pride, excess of food, and prosperous ease but did not aid the poor and needy. They were haughty and did abominable things before me; therefore I removed them when I saw it.*

(*Ezekiel 16:48-50*)

According to Ezekiel, Jerusalem had become a more unjust place than Sodom, whose sins he names as having abundance but ignoring those among them who were poor and needy, which was declared to be an abominable act. Note that the word *abomination* has a specific meaning in Hebrew. It's the word *towebah*, and it means something that is ritually or ethically impure for the Israelites (It doesn't always mean something is a sin, per se, but that for this particular people it is off limits). In Ezekiel 16, God names as *towebah* and condemns the people of Sodom for their failure to practice justice, not for their practice of same-sex love. The ego of Sodom was so inflated that it required a divine recalibration, Ezekiel says. For the prophets, Sodom is a warning to be heeded. When a people experience great abundance and have little compassion or care for those in need, trouble is coming.

When a people experience great abundance and have little compassion or care for those in need, trouble is coming

---

Next, we turn to the words of Jesus. I've heard many advocates, like me, of the full inclusion of the LGBTQ+ community in the life of the church say that Jesus never spoke about sexual orientation. That is true as far as I can tell. He does, however, mention Sodom. In Matthew 10 (and a similar passage in Luke 10), Jesus sent out his disciples to preach the good news that the Kingdom of Heaven had come near, and they were empowered to heal the sick, raise the dead, and exorcise unclean spirits. He also commanded that they not take money, nor should they pack for their travels. They were to enter the villages in which they would preach and depend on the hospitality of those communities to meet their needs. If they found themselves in a situation in which the community would not provide hospitality for them they were to "shake off the dust from [their] feet" as they left. He added, "Truly I tell you, it will be more tolerable for the land of Sodom and Gomorrah on the day of judgment than for that town" (Matthew 10:15).

Jesus's invocation of Sodom here is directly connected to how the disciples were to handle being refused hospitality by a community in which they had labored. This isn't an interpretive stretch, but, I think, the obvious connection between the work the disciples were being called to do and the potential for their work to go unappreciated. These villages were like Sodom because of their refusal to practice hospitality.

Taken together these texts support the reading of the Sodom story that I have offered in this chapter. The sin of Sodom was not same-sex love, but a total and complete lack of love and compassion toward those in need. They feared the stranger among them to such an extent that they began to behave with hostility toward them. As we listen to the witness of the prophets and Jesus, we also now turn to the central question raised by seeing this story within its context. What is the sin of Sodom today?

THE SIN OF SODOM TODAY

Every year my community, GracePointe Church in Nashville, Tennessee, participates in the annual Pride parade. We gather as a community and march to celebrate the beauty and belovedness of our Queer siblings. It's an event full of joy and hope. Alas, it never fails that at some point on the parade route there will be a small cluster of preachers with megaphones holding signs that declare the LGBTQ+ community to be sinful and under the judgment of God. It also never fails that, in those moments, there is a tragic irony present. The sin of Sodom was not, as we have seen, being Queer. The sin of Sodom was being hostile and inhospitable, much like the preachers with their signs and megaphones, condemning and excluding a community of God's beloved children.

The sin of Sodom is not a thing of the past, but something we are still very deeply wrestling with today. One of the theological struggles of our time is what place, if any, LGBTQ+ persons might have in the church community. Far too often the decision is that members of that community can attend and give their money, but any meaningful belonging is withheld from them. One of the texts cited for this posture is Genesis 19. To be sure there are other passages, known colloquially as the "Clobber Passages," and a full treatment of those texts stretches us beyond the scope of this book. I enthusiastically recommend the book *Unclobber: Rethinking Our Misuse of the Bible on Homosexuality* by my dear friend Colby Martin. It is an invaluable resource on these particular passages.

However, in this chapter we have seen how situating the story of Sodom in both the larger context of hospitality conventions in the ancient world and the larger canon of Scripture reveals a completely different emphasis. The way this story has been interpreted and weaponized, and used to exclude and marginalize our Queer siblings, is a textbook example of why context matters so greatly. While believing we were being faithful to the text we have actually done the opposite. As we have tried to avoid the sin of Sodom by excluding the LGBTQ+ community, we have actually committed that very sin. We have for too long been inhospitable and hostile, instead of opening our communities and providing hospitality. Now is the time for repentance. As my friend Stan Mitchell says, we aren't doing something magnanimous by including our LGBTQ+ siblings. We are stopping doing something awful. Our LGBTQ+ siblings belong at Jesus's table, and when understood in its ancient context, the story of Sodom doesn't challenge that truth. It confirms it.

Of course, this story's impact stretches even further, calling us as people of faith to the practice of hospitality toward all of God's children. The call of Scripture again and again directs our attention to the marginalized, oppressed, and vulnerable. How do we do this? How do we ensure that we are practicing the kind of compassion and hospitality that our tradition sees as our basic human responsibility? I will suggest a few places to begin.

I am more and more convinced that our budgets are moral documents. That is true for us as individuals, families, churches, and as a country. Are we prioritizing justice in the way we spend our money? Are the poor and marginalized forgotten? Are they simply given the leftover scraps of our spending or does the work of justice become a priority for us? These are key questions that should be at the center of our conversations around how we use our resources.

We are living in a time of heightened polarization in the United States, and one of the core tensions that is regularly being publicly debated and argued about is immigration. No one in Washington, DC, has asked for my policy ideas, but that does not mean there is nothing we can do. How can we as individuals or as churches work to be hospitable to the immigrants who reside among us? What are practical ways to make them feel welcomed and included in our communities? In a time of increased xenophobia in our country, how can our presence be one that neutralizes hate and fear, and offers love and inclusion?

Finally, what might it look like to practice hospitality toward people of other religious traditions? Or to people who have no faith tradition? When our posture toward those who believe or worship differently than we do is closed and hostile we cut ourselves off from so many potential benefits. Listening to and learning from someone of another tradition or no tradition isn't a threat to our own. On the contrary, it can be significantly enriching.

Listening to and learning from someone of another tradition or no tradition isn't a threat to our own.

In recent years some beautiful work has been done in Omaha, Nebraska, on this front. The Tri-Faith Initiative saw three communities, representing the three Abrahamic faiths, joined together to construct their buildings and a shared space on the same property. Temple Israel, Countryside Community Church (UCC), and the American Muslim Institute have created a beautiful example of different religious traditions working and playing well together. The Tri-Faith Initiative (trifaith.org) is breaking new, hospitable ground that is benefiting their members and the larger community in profound ways. As the world continues to grow smaller and smaller, and the hostilities of the world seem to grow larger and larger, it is all the more important for us to find ways to practice generous, open, and transformative hospitality that allows us to find common ground and leverage our resources and creativity to make the world a place where all human beings can flourish.

All of this, friends, is the work of the gospel. It's the work that we have been entrusted to carry on. As we lean into building larger tables, and not taller fences, we will discover the joy, creativity, and transformation that collaboration and hospitality generate. Added to that, we will also realize the repentance and healing of the past wounds that we have created through out-of-context misreadings of our Scripture. All of this and more become possible when we understand and commit ourselves to the value of hospitality.

POSTSCRIPT

Finding Our Place

"What does this mean for my life?"

In my religious upbringing, that was the most important question we could ask of any biblical text. We came to the Bible with the understanding that these poems, stories, and letters had something to say about our lives and the way we lived them. I still believe there is truth in that idea. Somehow, again and again, I find a wisdom, challenge, and vision that are relevant and meaningful, even after all this time. I know I'm not alone in that experience.

The Bible is a collection of texts, a library, that records for us some of the experiences of our spiritual ancestors. It is not the totality of their experience, we know. They didn't record everything, but what they did preserve for us gives us at least glimpses into their lives as they wrestled with similar questions about life, God, suffering, and humanity that we do today.

One of my favorite parts of engaging the Bible is connecting the dots between what the text says and the events of the time and place that led to the writing of those texts. As we've traveled through the six examples in this book, I am sure that has been more than obvious.

You could say I'm a bit of a history nerd. But we don't just read the Bible to learn about the past, do we? At some point we open the pages of Scripture hoping that somehow, someway, these ancient words can speak to our own moment. We are still reading the Bible after all this time because we hope that the past can impact and shape the present, and as a result, create a different future. So, as we conclude this study, let's spend a few moments on how we find ourselves in the pages of Scripture.

We are still reading the Bible after all this time because we hope that the past can impact and shape the present, and as a result, create a different future.

While it might sound counterintuitive, the first step toward finding our place in the Bible is to do exactly what we have done in this book. To reiterate that point, it's *context, context, context.* When we just begin with our world and our time we can end up misusing and misapplying Scripture in ways that are profoundly harmful.

There's a variously attributed adage that goes something like this: A text without context is a pretext. When we remove a passage or verse from a book of the Bible and give no attention to the realities of context that inspired and shaped that text, we can then distort and twist it to prove whatever point we want to make. When you're using the Ransom Note approach, if you recall from the Introduction, and you look long enough, it's possible to construct an argument for just about anything (even if the text was originally saying the exact opposite). I've found that to be true in my own experience. Looking back over my lifetime of interacting with the Bible I can now see how, especially early on, that my lack of contextual understanding led me to misapply and misuse the Bible in an attempt to prove my rightness. One embarrassing story from my know-it-all-youth might help illustrate this point.

I began preaching around the age of fifteen, and I immediately assumed, with no education or training, that I probably knew the Bible better than most other people in my life. The truth is that I didn't have a clue. That, however, did not stop me. I remember being in an argument with a friend in my youth group who was making some decision with which I had a problem. Honestly, they were probably listening to non-Christian music and I felt the need to stage an intervention. Regardless, they did not welcome my efforts. They felt like I was being judgmental (I was) and that whatever they were doing wasn't really my business (it wasn't). I was undaunted, and continued quoting random and out-of-context Bible verses to prove how right I was, and of equal importance, how wrong they were.

"Be in the world but not of the world," I said, referencing John 17.

"Do not be yoked with unbelievers," I pontificated, referencing (and misunderstanding) something Paul wrote to the Corinthians.

Finally, they tried to reason with me by quoting a passage from the Sermon on the Mount. "Do you remember," they asked, "when Jesus said to take the beam out of your eye before removing the speck in someone else's?"

I did remember that passage, but in my self-righteous bluster I offered what I thought Jesus really meant to say. "I've got the speck out of my eye," I declared, "and I am coming for the plank in yours!"

This would be a fantastic spot for a facepalm emoji, wouldn't it? Looking back on that encounter I am both completely embarrassed, both by my attitude and my approach to Scripture. Learning as much we can about the context of the author, original recipients, and even the history of interpretation of a passage can help us avoid these kind of regrettable misuses of the Bible.

Beginning with the context that produced a text then allows us to ask the question that we really want to ask, the question that causes us to come to the Bible in the first place: What is this saying to us, today? The more I study Scripture the more I feel a connection with the authors. While the world has changed in ways that would have been unfathomable to them—can you imagine taking them on an airplane or showing them an iPhone?—some things aren't all that different.

We are still living in a world where injustice is all too prevalent, where we decide who matters based on socioeconomic hierarchies, even within the Christian community. In many cases, a person's place in the community ends up being determined by the amount that they can contribute to the offering or the building program. Even two-thousand years later, Paul's words to the Corinthians, calling them to stop dividing up their community and making distinctions based on wealth, echo with relevance. As do Jesus's words, calling his disciples, then and now, to prioritize concern for the poor and the systems that keep people trapped in poverty.

Our current context also finds us grappling with biases and bigotries like xenophobia, homophobia, misogyny, and racism. We have no doubt had periods of progress in these areas, and it's so important to acknowledge that forward movement. However, if our present has taught us anything it's that we still have a long way to go in this area.

When we hear the subversive message of the Book of Ruth in this setting, it hasn't lost any of its edge and challenge. Nor has the story of Sodom and Gomorrah. While the cultures may differ, the call to be hospitable, to ensure the well-being of the stranger and marginalized among us, still needs to be answered by us.

The call to be hospitable, to ensure the well-being of the stranger and marginalized among us, still needs to be answered by us.

The world we know today can bring difficulty and challenges into our lives that we didn't expect. We find ourselves looking for hope, for a sense of belonging, and for someone to walk through the challenges of life alongside us. Surely Jeremiah and Paul didn't have us in mind when they wrote their respective letters, but we are the beneficiaries of their visions of God and community. For all the differences between our ancient spiritual ancestors and us, we really aren't all that different, are we?

A contextual reading of Scripture becomes a place for us in which the past meets the present. That, then, becomes the context in which we will decide what we will do to create a better future. Listening to how these stories and songs from the past speak to our moment is only part of the work. We must also embrace the invitation to live differently in response to what we learn. The point isn't just to know what mistakes our spiritual ancestors made, but to benefit from their experience and make better choices. We don't just hear about their experiences of God as a substitute for ours, but we learn from them and allow them to help us cultivate an awareness of God for ourselves in our own moment.

Helping us find our place in the Bible is really why I wrote this book. One of the concerns I often hear from people when I talk about the importance of contextual work is the sense of being overwhelmed.

"Where do we even begin?" they ask.

This is an important question. After all, not everyone has the time or opportunity to, say, pursue a graduate or post-graduate degree in the Bible. Fortunately, we don't need to start there. If I could offer one piece of advice or encouragement it would be this: Pay attention.

One of my favorite stories in all of Scripture is Moses's encounter of God at the burning bush in Exodus chapter 3. Moses, who by this point has quite the backstory, is a shepherd, tending his father-in-law's herds. On what I imagine to be a pretty routine, normal day, out of the corner of his eye, Moses catches a glimpse of something confusing. It was a bush that was on fire, but not consumed. A burning bush might not have been an oddity in his world, but a burning-but-not-consumed bush definitely was. It was too much. His curiosity got the better of him.

"Then Moses said, 'I must turn aside and look at this great sight and see why the bush is not burned up'" (Exodus 3:3).

Moses listened to his curiosity, and it changed not only the course of Jewish history, but the history of humanity as a whole.

When I say, "pay attention," I mean to be attuned to what comes before and after a specific passage. As we've seen with the author of Mark's use of intercalation, or sandwiches, what comes before and after a text has significant importance for interpreting the meaning of a particular passage. This is also true of seeing a passage and book in the larger context of the rest of the biblical canon. How does this passage resonate or push back on other texts in the rest of Scripture? Being aware of how the biblical authors interact with one another is immensely helpful.

Additionally, as you read the Bible, notice what stands out to you. Does something inspire your curiosity? Do you notice some sort of contradiction, for example, in the way a person or place is named or described? Is there a detail that you caught this time that you overlooked last time? What questions are raised by your reading? I recommend writing it all down, so you have a record of what struck you while you were reading. Then you can begin the search for resources that can help begin to give shape and context to your questions. I've found the process to be endlessly interesting, exciting, and transformative. I hope you do too.

Read the Bible for the First Time— Again.

In *Bible Stories for Grown-Ups: Reading Scripture with New Eyes* pastor Josh Scott looks at familiar Bible stories and reveals new details and interpretations for an adult audience. This six-week Bible study considers stories many read as children including Noah's Ark, the binding of Isaac, Jonah and the big fish, Jesus and Zacchaeus, Jesus healing a blind man, and the parable of the talents. Scott reimagines these stories and opens new visions for readers to understand well-known pieces of Scripture in our current cultural environment.

The book can be read alone or used by small groups and can be used anytime throughout the year. Additional components include video teaching sessions featuring Josh Scott, and a comprehensive leader guide, making this perfect as a six-week group study done throughout the year.

ISBN 978-1-7910-2662-2

Also available Leader Guide (ISBN 978-1-7910-2664-6)
and DVD (ISBN 978-1-7910-2666-0)

Available wherever fine books are sold.

Watch videos based on *Context: Putting Scripture in Its Place* with Josh Scott through Amplify Media.

Amplify Media is a multimedia platform that delivers high quality, searchable content with an emphasis on Wesleyan perspectives for churchwide, group, or individual use on any device at any time. In a world of sometimes overwhelming choices, Amplify gives church leaders and congregants media capabilities that are contemporary, relevant, effective, and, most importantly, affordable and sustainable.

With *Amplify Media* church leaders can:

- Provide a reliable source of Christian content through a Wesleyan lens for teaching, training, and inspiration in a customizable library
- Deliver their own preaching and worship content in a way the congregation knows and appreciates
- Build the church's capacity to innovate with engaging content and accessible technology
- Equip the congregation to better understand the Bible and its application
- Deepen discipleship beyond the church walls

⋀ AMPLIFY. MEDIA

Ask your group leader or pastor about Amplify Media and sign up today at www.AmplifyMedia.com.